VIETNAM
EVEN GOD IS AGAINST US

WRITTEN, ORIGINAL PAINTINGS,
PHOTOGRAPHY, DRAWINGS AND SCULPTURE
BY

AUSTIN DEUEL

PUBLISHED BY IMPRESSIONS WEST

PUBLISHED IN THE UNITED STATES OF AMERICA
IMPRESSIONS WEST
847 NORTH METCALF STREET
ESCONDIDO, CALIFORNIA 92025

DEDICATION

I dedicate this book to all the men who left the silent, empty chairs at their twenty year high school reunions, leaving behind friends to remember them; and to the men who left families without fathers and sons, leaving behind loved ones to honor them. Each loss marking a personal sacrifice to the Vietnam War.

ILLUSTRATIONS

Map of Vietnam, *watercolor*	XIII
Night Flares Across From Da Nang, *watercolor*	17
Second Plane In, *watercolor*	19
Da Nang, *watercolor*	21
Cooling Off, *bronze*	25
Marble Mountain, *watercolor*	27
Coming Home, *watercolor*	29
CA-C D6; Hoi An, *watercolor*	31
Incoming Wounded, *watercolor*	33
Unsung Heroes, *watercolor*	35
Fire Mission, *watercolor*	37
Reinforcements-Union II; Khe Sanh, *watercolor*	39
First Volley, *oil*	43
Answering The Call For Ammo, *oil*	45
Good Bye, Dear Friend, *watercolor*	47
Ticket Out, *oil*	49
Returning Fire, *watercolor*	51
Support Fire; Hill 881 South, *watercolor*	53
Cold And Wet, *watercolor*	55
Big Guns Moving In, *watercolor*	57
Even God Is Against Us, *oil*	58, 59
A Moment Of Peace, *bronze*	63
The Girls Of CIB, *watercolor*	67
Downtown Saigon, *watercolor*	71
Boys Will Be Boys, *watercolor*	77
Intruder, *watercolor*	79
Long Hours, Little Pay, *watercolor*	81
Fire Power On The Move, *watercolor*	83
Helping Hands, *watercolor*	85
Medivac; Operation Hickory, *watercolor*	87
Truckload For The Gods, *watercolor*	89
Looking Across The River From CIB, *watercolor*	93
Symbols Of 1967, *collage*	99
Held Back By The Chains Of Politics, *watercolor*	113
For What; Hill 881 South, *bronze*	115
The Victims, *watercolor*	119
The Marine's Marine, *watercolor*	123
Vietnam War Memorial, San Antonio, *bronze*	129
Final Tribute, Twenty Years Later, *watercolor*	131

INTRODUCTION

This book is short, but if a picture is worth a thousand words then it is as long as "War and Peace."

Vietnam is a tough subject to cover properly, as well as a highly emotional one for those who lived during that time in our country's history. Serving in Vietnam, the Marine Corps and every other branch of our military service did the job given them and did it well. As enlisted men and officers, the young men of this country went to Vietnam well trained and with the highest average education level of any group the United States has ever assembled to fight a war. Their courage under hostile fire was beyond dispute. The only questionable areas concern the purpose and politics of a long war that was triggered by the still highly debatable credibility of events that transpired one night in the Tonkin Gulf.

The twentieth century is now slipping away into the history books by which succeeding generations will judge the successes and failures of this 100-year span. World War II, at the halfway mark, brought an end to war as the world had known it up until then. Earlier wars involved full-out, direct invasion of territory with the single purpose of conquering and possessing the invaded land. Such an invasion was often slowed down by guerilla warfare but if no significant help came from another large power, the conqueror stayed, was assimilated into the conquered system, and life went on.

Today's conflicts start with guerrilla warfare because the causes are ideological differences regarding form of government and who should be in control. The opposing opinions are backed half-heartedly by one or the other of the world's two super powers, each of whom has backed the incumbent or challenger in different areas of the world, depending on which they agree with or want in power to enhance their own global position.

For the United States, this change in tactics has taken place since Korea. We have interfered directly or indirectly all over the world, actions launched by the hysterical efforts of the McCarthy era to "stop the red tide that is covering the globe." Today, "human rights violations" give us our excuse for the interference that causes suffering and death for a lot more people than it sets free, as we found out in Vietnam. But we are not alone. The Russians have Afghanistan for their lesson, the Jews have Lebanon, the French have Indochina and Algiers, and the British have India.

Many parts of the world are in conflict right now because of ideological differences. Having the super powers choose sides and then make half-hearted contributions to their political favorites only prolongs this internal strife. Vietnam was the longest war we ever fought in, and we lost. Israel has been fighting since 1948, branching out from its initial plan of occupation until there is no end in sight. The Russian revolution didn't take as long as the campaign to control Afghanistan by means of limited commitment to a puppet government, and this will probably continue until either home pressure forces them to leave or they mount an all-out invasion and occupation as they did in Poland, Czechoslovakia and Hungary.

These wars are costly to all those involved, and last much longer than old-fashioned wars where the technique was to conquer in an all-out effort or be driven back into the sea. The suffering of the populace is extended by many years, and the decimation of families is irreparable. Ordinary people, with neither stake nor say in these ideological battles, are the real victims. Our Vietnam venture caused terrible suffering during the years we were involved, and will continue doing so until those who were unwilling pawns in this game without rules have passed on to escape the lingering effects of its devastation.

Those who believed our intentions of seeing the war in southeast Asia through instead of quitting left our soldiers to bear the burden of our government's misgivings, tainting their characters for going and having their wartime actions interpreted as "murder." The South Vietnamese who chose to work for a cause exposed their preference for a government they thought we would never abandon in its struggle. But we did, and left them to a fate of long imprisonment, torture, even execution. Some of those who survived all this escaped in small, over-crowded boats, only to land in some distant refugee camp or drift up on some country's shore and be refused entry as illegal immigrants — this, after an incredible human effort stemming from the desperation of the situation in which we had left them.

The South Vietnamese, along with many other refugees from similar conflicts, wait in these camps located throughout the world. Their children are growing up in the camps, and those who survive to be the next generation will only know the smell of death and burnt gunpowder; the sound of a helicopter or jet will send them scurrying, and not because they are late for a flight to Acapulco. Their hearts will be sealed in hate and the strongest will have to be dealt with someday. These types of "no-win" wars and the refugee camps they spawn have given rise to violence-prone minds and temperaments, and the fault lies with the super powers' penchant for interfering in other nation's governments in order to further their own political objectives. The people thus affected will rise out of a dark fear and frustration to demand an immediate policy change; failing that, a "nothing to lose" violence will ensue.

This book is about one such war and its tragic aftermath that continues to this day. I do hope that as the veterans of this era come into positions of power and policy-making, they will not forget the lesson and fall back into the vacillating attitudes of the past. In the future, we should be careful in our commitments, but if we commit, we should see it through to the end.

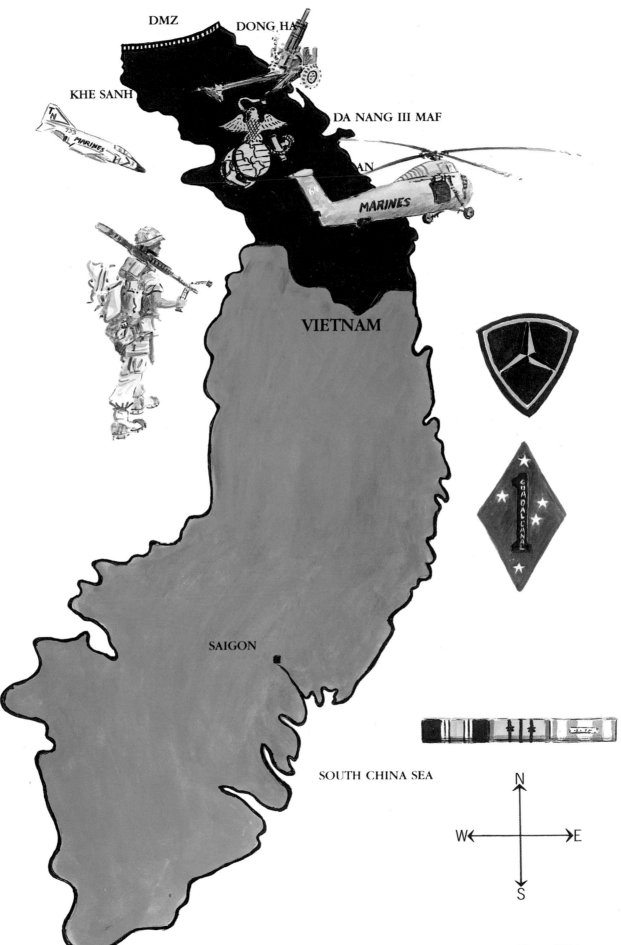

DMZ

DONG HA

KHE SANH

DA NANG III MAF

MARINES

MARINES

VIETNAM

SAIGON

GUADALCANAL

SOUTH CHINA SEA

N

W←→E

S

Map of Vietnam   XIII

The Vietnam War brought death and loss of limb to its young soldiers, but that was its only similarity to any other war in our country's history with the possible exception of the American Indian Wars during which women, children and their homes were considered military targets. But those soldiers returned home as heroes — not as "baby killers" to a country that denied the validity of their efforts and marred their homecoming with insults or apathy.

The reason for my personal exposure to Vietnam was different than that of most Vietnam participants during those trying times for our country and its people, and it transpired through a series of unusual events. I was to attend this theater of action for a little over three months as a Marine Combat Artist. But, belying that designation, my experiences with war would be complete and intense, both physically and emotionally; the after-effects, the coming home experience, were to compare with those of many others who went.

It all began because of a great childhood interest in the West. I was exposed to Western art as a teenager in Pennsylvania through magazines. Paintings by Charles Russell and Frederic Remington caught my eye and fancy. A lot of their paintings appeared in full page advertisements in *Life* and *Saturday Evening Post* in the 1950's (for products such as Sunnybrook Whiskey) which would list the source as "Courtesy of the Boston Museum of Art." I would write the museum, or any other source I stumbled across, for copies. My parents supported this interest by having them framed for me on occasions such as my birthday or Christmas.

At the age of twenty-five, I visited the Death Valley Art Show in Death Valley, California, and made up my mind to return the next year and make my debut as a Western artist. The Death Valley Art Show has been in existence since 1949 and is responsible for launching many an art career since it is the only major contemporary Western Art show in the United States open to new artists trying to show their works to an interested public. It was the watering hole for those who thirsted for Western art before its acceptance in the major art galleries and over-all market, and many of today's famous Western artists passed through this show at one time or another. The Death Valley Art Show is still in existence, and although it no longer is the only annual Western Art show, it is the oldest in America. It includes an invitational art show in the Death Valley Museum, along with an open show in the parking lot and on the lawn fronting the museum.

The open show is for those willing to drive hundreds of miles and set out their works for public viewing and purchase. In November, 1966, this is where I started along with many others, with high hopes of being invited to the prestigious inside show at some time in the coming years. There was an outside competition based on public vote so winning any ribbon in that helped in the cause of reaching your ultimate goal. The artists came from all over, and we slept in the backs of cars or pickup trucks, or in sleeping bags on the ground, waiting for our art careers to blossom so we could afford motor homes or a stay at the motel with the more successful artists.

Due to the distance I had to travel, I arrived a little late. While still setting up panels on which to hang my art, items started selling. In the midst of selling almost everything, I received a commission for three large paintings for Stove Pipe Wells Restaurant and Motel, located in the middle of Death Valley. This being my very first art show, I had expected little acceptance and I was stunned, almost in a daze, at my success.

To top it off, one woman who had shown interest in my work returned at the end of the show and asked me if I would like to be a combat artist for the Navy. I became very excited and said, "Of course! I would be honored."

She wrote a note for me to give to the Information Officer at China Lake Navy Base which I would drive by on my way home to San Diego.

The next day I stopped at China Lake, note in hand. The Information Officer was able to see me immediately. I introduced myself and we discussed the purpose of my visit. He liked my work but, officially, it had to be approved by the Municipal Art Director of the City of Los Angeles. Once that was accomplished, there would be no problem arranging the combat art assignment. In retrospect, I have no idea why the U.S. Navy deferred to the City of Los Angeles for approval of its combat art program.

A few days later I was standing in the Art Director's office, nervous as a cat. He gave the work quite a look and it seemed an eternity before he gave me an answer of approval. I was ecstatic, but things started to crumble as the conversation progressed and he explained the Navy's program, showing me some of the paintings that had been done for this program. He told me I would be going as a civilian but with a rating, as far as privileges and freedom were concerned, equivalent to that of a full colonel in the Marines. But the paintings I was viewing disturbed me. They were of cocktail parties, the inside of a jet cockpit, water buffaloes plowing a field in the Philippines. It didn't look much like combat art to me.

I explained that I wanted to get closer to combat than the scenes these paintings depicted; I wanted personal contact with the war. I also told him that I had been in the Marine Corps and had some basic training for this experience. I was not interested in painting ships at the dock or aircraft carriers steaming off the coast of Vietnam or activities on a flight line at an airbase. I wanted to go on combat patrols with a Seal Team, or on a small river boat on patrol. I said I thought that the whole idea and purpose of a combat artist was to cover the real thing. He explained that because I would be a civilian under Navy jurisdiction they could not expose me to combat due to the liability factor. I said I would sign any waiver necessary to release them from responsibility for my well-being. He still maintained he could not guarantee to get me any closer to the war than Saigon or a large Navy vessel off the coast of Vietnam. I was disappointed, to say the least, but decided to let him proceed with the necessary paperwork to get me that far, thinking if I got that close I could work out the rest.

Heading for home just north of San Diego, I was frustrated at the way the meeting had gone and the so-called "combat art" I had witnessed. You didn't have to leave the States to paint pictures like that! The Marine Corps base at Camp Pendleton was abreast of me on the freeway and I had a sudden urge to drive in. I asked the MP at the gate for directions to the Combat Information Bureau (CIB) building. Finding it, I walked in and approached a lance corporal standing behind the counter. I blurted out, "Do you people need a combat artist?"

For an instant an "are you crazy?" look appeared in his eyes but he disappeared into an office to repeat the question to a higher authority.

A short time passed as I stared around the room of dark green metal filing cabinets, dark brown desks, battleship gray walls, with shiny Marines working unnatural weapons — typewriters — and staring at the manila folders surrounding them. Then the young corporal returned with a lieutenant who said, "You're not going to believe this, but I just received a request from

Marine Corps Headquarters to find an artist among our ranks for the purpose of being a combat artist in Vietnam."

I immediately said, "I'll be one."

I thought I was what they classify as a Class Three Reservist since I had never received my final discharge from the Marine Corps and all they would have to do was order me to active duty. I had just turned twenty-seven and I had joined the Marine Corps at twenty, so the time element was right to be in that classification. The lieutenant agreed, but first we had to send photographs of my work to Washington for approval and, if that was received, go forward with the necessary details to acquire my orders for active duty status.

My work was approved but one little hitch arose: they discovered my final discharge was in my file; it had just never been sent to me.

"Okay," I said, "I'll join a Marine Corps reserve unit and you can order me to active duty from there."

They said that would be fine so I went to San Diego and joined a tank unit at Miramar Naval Air Station. I finally received my orders and could hardly believe my good fortune.

I had not told my wife anything about this effort to realize my goal, feeling it was no use worrying anyone until the effort became fact. I also wanted to take out a $50,000 life insurance policy and the salesman thought I was nuts because I had him eliminate the clause covering non-payment in the event of death due to acts of war. He knew nothing of my plans to rejoin the Marine Corps. I know today they would not have paid off in the event of my death in Vietnam, but it was one of those youthful tries at covering all bases and it would possibly make my wife feel better at the security level with which all women are concerned. I foresaw that one reaction when I dropped the bomb would be, "What am I going to do if you don't come back home?"

I went home and announced I had rejoined the Marine Corps, would be going to Washington in March, then would return and go to Vietnam in April. I don't think anyone believed me at first; the reaction was silent shock.

DO YOU GUYS NEED A COMBAT ARTIST!

Most combat artists in earlier wars were attached to Marine Corps magazines such as *The Leatherneck* for enlisted men and *The Gazette* for officers. Their artwork was done and published at Marine Corps Headquarters in Washington, D.C. Colonel Henri was now head of this program and it was his conception to send artists into the field to work from their studios in a war zone. The Marine Corps had never before in its history had such a program as this in wartime. Colonel Henri fought for the budget and the validity of the plan and got the travel authorizations needed to move in Vietnam. He also handpicked the artists he wanted for this unique program.

I flew to Washington in March to be briefed on what was expected of me as the first enlisted man to be placed in this new program. When I finally arrived and walked through the front door of Marine Corps Headquarters' Henderson Hall, I was met by a large painting by ex-marine Joe Grandee of Ira Hayes in traditional Indian clothes and mounted on a great paint horse. In the sky above him, ghostlike figures portrayed the flag-raising on Iwo Jima. It seemed the ultimate of Marine Corps tradition.

The first person I met in the program was Major Leahy who had recently come aboard after leaving his position as an instructor at the Famous Artists School started by Norman Rockwell, Harold von Schmidt, Albert Dorne, and a few other famous illustrators of our time. I had taken the course but never finished it. Colonel Henri had come from a job as art director for an advertising agency in New York City. All in the program had excellent art backgrounds.

One of my first jobs was to round up and organize existing original Marine Corps art from past wars, catalog it, and place it in the first Marine Corps Art Gallery, a room requisitioned by Colonel Henri for this purpose. Up to this point, due to lack of organization and control, much of the art depicting Marine Corps history was lost. Thanks to Colonel Henri, concern for it was revived and a program established to protect it.

As I started my quest for art, which was scattered around various Headquarters offices, I couldn't believe the works I was discovering and handling. I came upon Tom Lovell originals, the first I had ever seen. He was one of the artistic heroes from my teen years. I used to cut his work out of *Life* and the *National Geographic*, frame it and save it for my art files long before I ever found out he had been a Marine sergeant at one time. I discovered that fact in boot camp at Parris Island in 1959; his framed prints hung on the bulkheads in the mess halls. I immediately recognized his work and signature, but the "sergeant" in front of the name was a surprise.

During my treasure hunt through Marine Headquarters, I came across other works I enjoyed, paintings by Howard Brodie and John Groth, Joe Grandee's painting of Ira Hayes as the Pima Indian who went to war. It was a great opportunity for a young artist to be able to examine and handle such quality work.

The earlier discovery of some of these artists had rekindled my interest in art. I had put it on the shelf after my disastrous brush with art school and the art world in Trenton, New Jersey, where I did window decorating by day and attended art school at night. I had quit in disgust, believing all artists were of the third sex, and the idea of "good art" that the school was pushing did not appeal to my instinct of what I like in painting. I didn't want to associate with those at the school or put up with the pressure of learning what "good art" is. Tom Lovell was what appealed to me and I knew you could be a normal man, too.

I preferred the more traditional approach to art, or good impressionism or good drawing. Colonel Henri liked, for lack of a better word, an "artier" approach. I remember I picked up a little painting, done in gray gouache medium, of Marines charging off the beach with Corsairs screaming overhead, guns blazing toward the enemy line before them. It was well drawn in a traditional manner with strong composition. I said, "Boy, I sure like this!"

Colonel Henri gave me a quick look and said, "That's West Coast poor taste."

I knew it was a little John Wayne-ish looking, but sometimes I'm in the mood for John Wayne. And I didn't have the heart to tell the colonel I had grown up in the East! Though our tastes at times were completely different, I admired him for making a very historical move and a positive one for the preservation of Marine Corps visual history.

My mind was totally art-oriented and I forgot I was in the Marine Corps. But from time to time the class system would sneak up on me and create some humorous situations, due to my very effective rank of Private First Class. While walking the corridors of Henderson Hall, I dressed in college-type civilian clothes. Unless someone saw my orders, I was treated well and the barriers were less restrictive to my movements in pursuit of my job. When the occasion did arise when I was forced to produce my orders, my standard of living was reduced considerably.

My first night I had to make arrangements for temporary billeting. I walked into an office to get a bunk assignment and draw linen. A sergeant behind the counter was handing out everything, including advice. I stood there, 6'3" in my Ivy League sportcoat, and asked for a rack and some linen, please.

"Oh, yes sir, get it right away. May I see your orders, sir?"

I handed over the large manila envelope. He opened it, looked at me, then said abruptly, "Sit over there," and disappeared.

About twenty minutes later, a lance corporal returned with a blanket and sheets and the information as to where I could apply the well-known military skill of making a bunk. I began to feel like an undercover cop whose badge just fell out of his pocket, and knew that as I got deeper into the Marine Corps world, away from Headquarters, it was going to get worse for me.

Two weeks later, I left Washington, headed for home and then my assignment. After seeing so much great art work, I was even more excited about the opportunity I'd been given. My orders from Colonel Henri were to be a Marine first and an artist second; he didn't want the artistic privilege abused. He had already had some complaints from Vietnam that people in the program were more "artistic" than "military" in character. Colonel Henri wanted these problems corrected and our program recognized as part of the team, not an independent power trip. He advised me I could paint anything I wanted, and authorized me to buy the art supplies that would be necessary to achieve this. Major Leahy's parting remark was to remind me this would probably be the most important opportunity and experience in my life. In the early years after my return from Vietnam, his statement was buried beneath subsequent sad events, but twenty years later fate handed me the opportunity to make Major Leahy's prophecy come true.

I arrived home, arranged for the needed art supplies, and waited anxiously for my definite departure date for Vietnam. During this period I met a "bird" colonel, Colonel Stiff, who was coming back on active duty for the combat art program; we would be traveling together to Vietnam. He lived near my art gallery at Lake San Marcos. We talked of the new program we were about to embark on and his art background. Also, by chance, the colonel met a friend of mine who was selling me picture frames for my paintings. Larry had given me his World War II Marine Corps ring for luck in Vietnam. He had switched this ring with his best friend in the Marine Corps just before they both left for the South Pacific. They both had made it back so he was passing the luck on to me. During this accidental meeting of the colonel and Larry, it turned out that Larry's best friend was in Colonel Stiff's platoon when he was a young lieutenant in the South Pacific theater of action. Larry's friend had even written an ode to then-Lieutenant Stiff, citing his value as a leader under fire and his exceptional gallantry. Larry still remembered it, to Colonel Stiff's embarrassment.

The colonel was a very quiet and reserved man; Larry was loud and outgoing and did most of the reminiscing about their mutual experiences in the South Pacific. Larry dramatically related an experience to the colonel to see if he remembered it. It seems the Japanese had built a submarine pen on one of the very small islands in the South Pacific campaign area in which they were both involved. Larry was demolition and he and six other Marines were sent in to blow the doors off of it. Larry asked the colonel if he remembered that explosion. The colonel replied, "Yes! You killed more Marines than you did Japs!"

It seems that when they set the charges on the doors they forgot to allow for the fact that the Japanese torpedoes stored inside would add to their explosion in a chain reaction, so what ensued was a tremendous surprise. The force killed or wounded all those involved, including Larry, and sent debris hurtling through the air to land on other nearby islands and injure more Marines.

CHAPTER THREE

The big day finally arrived. I received my orders to report to CIB at Camp Pendleton at 0700 to start my briefing, shots, physical, and various classes to complete the staging process for the adventure that lay before me. I was there at the appointed time, meeting Colonel Stiff and Lt. Colonel Hunter. After brief greetings, the colonel and I headed for a four-door green Chevrolet and driver. As the colonel reached for the door I remembered, all of a sudden, that there was a military protocol for this situation covering who gets in or out first, according to rank — and I couldn't remember the proper order. I knew then I was going to be in trouble before the day was over. I'm also sure I was the only PFC ever driven through staging in the back seat of a car with a "bird" colonel. Even the driver outranked me! Fortunately, I didn't have any rank visible on my utilities to expose my true station in the Marine Corps community. It remained camouflaged in green and unquestioned so long as I was within hand-holding distance of the colonel.

The colonel gave all the directions to the driver. As we whisked around Camp Pendleton, he chose the classes of briefings he was interested in, passing up the ones he wasn't. In place of the ones he decided to skip, he would use the time to look up an old command or friend. Each time the Chevy came to rest, we would get out in the hail of "snapping to" and salutes which always accompany the arrival of brass. I was much stared at and stayed close to the colonel to keep from having to answer questions regarding my relationship to the colonel or the situation. I was praying they wouldn't discover my true identity. In making the colonel comfortable, one captain we were visiting was handing me coffee and refills right along with the colonel's. I knew it was just going to be a matter of time before this was going to blow.

One demonstration we did make was the rifle range for familiarity firing of the M-16, which was a brand-new weapon for the Marine Corps. I stepped out of the car behind the colonel into the midst of a half-dozen gunnery and staff sergeants who were standing by to demonstrate this new rifle for him. After a very smart military welcome, I became the object of the first really serious stares questioning my position in all of this, but I was too close to the colonel for immediate inquisition. A crisp redheaded sergeant stepped forward with the M-16 in his hand. He was a poster Marine with chiseled jaw and starched utilities. He sharply executed a "port arms" and ran off the nomenclature and the muzzle velocity and rounds per minute in brisk, military fashion.

The colonel snapped it out of his hands, inspected it with experienced eyes, then returned it to the sergeant who was waiting at attention.

"Does it jam, Sergeant?"

"Oh, no sir!" was the quick reply. "Would the Colonel like to step up to the firing line?"

The colonel stepped up and was again handed the rifle. He aimed down range and squeezed off three rounds semi-automatic, only to have it seize up on the fourth. I choked back a laugh.

The colonel turned, handed the weapon to the sergeant, and said, "That's what I thought."

This weapon was new and had a controversial reputation that it had just upheld.

They all headed off to the rifle rack to tear the rifle down and correct the problem of its malfunction. Unfortunately, the correction would be only temporary. I had become mesmerized by all this and forgot to stay close to the colonel. Before I knew it, I was surrounded by five sergeants with fiery eyes, demanding to know who the hell I was. To answer was death but they became more and more hostile in their tone and very impatient for my answer. Noticing my predicament, the colonel walked back and stepped into the circle to retrieve me. I felt like a cornered cat being saved from a pack of dogs. Needless to say, I was more careful from then on to stay close to the colonel so as to not duplicate that situation.

The colonel and I returned to CIB at five o'clock and said our goodbyes until the next morning. In parting, Colonel Hunter advised me that a master sergeant at Headquarters wanted to see me before I left. When I reported to the sergeant, he was very put out and started screaming at me, reminding me of my social position as a PFC in the Marine Corps. He advised me that my orders had said to report to Headquarters at 0700 and that was exactly what I should have done.

As soon as I got over my surprise at his wrath, I said, "Just a minute! First of all, I advised both Colonel Stiff and Lt. Colonel Hunter of the instructions in my orders. They told me to get in the car and take care of it later. Unless you outrank a colonel, and I certainly don't, you do as you're told. You can take the matter up with them."

He remained highly irritated, but he finally let me go. As I left, I knew this Marine Corps experience was going to be a seesaw affair.

The next few days were taken up with shots, physicals, and a trip down the Camp Pendleton version of the Ho Chi Minh Trail (showing off the ingenuity of an enemy that had little technology but lots of nasty ways to hurt you). There were no further incidents involving the social strata of the Marine Corps. I was becoming as tricky as the Viet Cong at hiding my identity.

I nervously started my day of departure standing at El Toro Marine Corps Air Base waiting to board the "big bird with the golden tail" — a Continental Airlines plane. What a way to go to war: a commercial airline and one that, before the anti-sexist laws, had the slogan, "We really move our tail for you." I stood with my wife, kids and father, staring at a formation of Marines diminishing its ranks one at a time as each name was called for boarding. As realization began to set in, a shudder passed through my body; this could be a passage to death or injury. I erased the thought immediately, feeling guilty. When my turn came, I kissed my wife and kids, shook hands with my father, and headed for an innocent, almost carefree mode of transportation carrying its cargo off to keep a date with possible death and destruction.

On the plane, the colonel and I were the only ones in summer dress uniforms. The rest wore freshly starched utilities of dark green, with a bit of bright white T-shirt showing at the neck. It was odd watching the stewardesses maneuver through the dark green mass of men like attending angels — this was definitely a war of contrasts. We took off, soaring out over the soft green hills of Laguna dotted with expensive dwellings, their pools reflecting the clear blue sky of that California afternoon.

We chased the sun for hours, which slowed its time of descent and created a sunset in slow motion until finally the giant fireball sank below the horizon, leaving a lingering afterglow like a dying campfire in the Old West. We arrived at Okinawa at 1:30 in the morning, having had only one brief stop in Honolulu to break the long flight.

When the colonel and I deplaned, we were met at the bottom of the stairs by two young corporals dressed in summer dress blues, their brilliant white caps standing out in the darkness like lighthouses on a dark coastline. They pointed the way to a patiently waiting green Chevy, accented in yellow letters and numbers, for our trip to the VIP room at Kadena airport. They advised the colonel they would retrieve our seabags from the belly of the 707. I thought this was going to be a bit of a needle-in-the-haystack chore, trying to distinguish our dark green seabags from all the others while maintaining the creases in their uniforms on this warm, humid night. In their eagerness to please the colonel and avoid any ire from high brass, they missed my PFC stripe hiding in the dark as they started their frantic search. The colonel had one and I had two seabags; one of my bags was filled with over a hundred pounds of art supplies, so after finding it they made several attempts before releasing it from its resting place. A bit out of breath, they dropped their find into the trunk of the car, resting the lid on the bulging load, then held the rear door open for the colonel and me. I passed by them to get into the back seat but they didn't notice my rank. They closed the door and we sped across the concrete runway toward the VIP room.

We came to an abrupt stop in front of a single door with one light overhead, its downward rays marking the entrance to this haven for the privileged. The two young men jumped to the immediate task of holding doors and unloading the trunk. But as I passed through the door into the bright lights of the room, my stripe was finally exposed to two very surprised Marines. Their reaction was pure instinct, each grabbing an arm to show me the exit in a manner very unlike my entrance. As I hit the main terminal, my seabags followed me with even less dignity.

Colonel Stiff glanced after me, but said only, "I'll see you in the morning, Austin."

I said, "Yes, sir," feeling like a black guy at a KKK meeting whose hood had just fallen off.

There was a sergeant observing all of this, resting on one of those ubiquitous military counters.

"What was that all about?" he asked.

I knew I was looking stupid as I tried to figure out my next move. I told him it was a long story and he said he had all night. He was in charge of emergency leave orders for persons coming out of Vietnam, keeping them moving as fast as possible to their destinations. So I told him the whole story of my assignment and where I was heading. He was very amused. He said if I wanted a rack that night I could go across the street to the Air Force as they had an enlisted men's BQ.

I thanked him and stood around for awhile, trying to decide whether to sit in one of the brown chairs with chrome arms and try to sleep there or take the sergeant's advice. As I wavered, I heard a voice calling "Private!" over and over. I looked around and spotted a major trying to get my attention. When he had caught my eye, he said, "Come over here, Private," so over I went.

"How old are you?" he asked.

When I answered twenty-seven, he said, "How come you're only a private?"

Oh boy, here we go again. I repeated what was becoming my stock phrase, "It's a long story."

At this rate, I could see I was going to have to write it down and be prepared to hand it out. He asked about my ribbons. I had only two, one a National Defense ribbon, but he was interested in the other, the Reserve Conduct ribbon.

He said, "You don't deserve it; take it off. When's the last time you qualified with a rifle?"

I replied, "A few years ago," so he made me take off my Expert's badge.

This sure was turning into a TV series. I had only been in Okinawa an hour and my reception wasn't going so well. I was beginning to think I should have gone with the Navy.

I decided to leave for safety's sake and go over to the Air Force BQ. There was only one thing left they could do: arrest me for being a PFC. I made it there without further encounters but I was almost afraid to request a rack. I had been thrown out of the VIP room, publicly stripped of my medals, and it wasn't even light yet on my first day out of the country!

Once bedded down, I couldn't sleep. So I picked up a book Colonel Stiff had given me called "Fix Bayonets", written and illustrated by a Captain Thomason during World War I. It described his personal experiences in the trenches of France. As a line officer, he ran an infantry company, yet found time to keep up with his diary and drawings. The colonel's interest in the book had started years earlier when he was an art student in the east, studying under Harvey Dunn, an artist as famous then as he is today. Dunn had also served in the Army during World War I as a captain and combat artist.

World War II broke out while Colonel Stiff was attending Dunn's class so he joined the Marine Corps from art school, figuring he, too, could describe his combat experiences with words and pictures as they were happening. But having been sent to the South Pacific, his great responsibilities and the long hours they entailed left no time for such an on-the-spot effort. Eventually, he became a career Marine instead of returning to the art world after the war. But he had always admired Captain Thomason's book and very kindly loaned it to me to help in my approach to the work ahead of me.

I finished the book but still couldn't sleep. So I got up, went out and just started walking around. It was light now and I had my sketchbook with me. I sat on the side of a road and started drawing some of the local farmers who were working their fields. After awhile, I moved on and came across an older Oriental man laying a cinder-block wall. The cinder-block was the only modern ingredient in the process. The man was dressed in baggy pants rolled above his knees, a cone-shaped straw hat and sandals. He had no plumb line or level, only crude wooden tools, and the wall was as crooked as a snake. I couldn't believe this was 1967 — that things could still be so primitive after we Americans had been on the island for more than twenty years.

Later in town, I saw Toyota cement trucks backed up to a highrise building, dumping their loads into grass baskets. These were then carried on native women's heads as they climbed scaffolding made of bamboo with rope-tied support joints. It was like watching a submarine putting supplies aboard a sailing ship.

I headed back to Kadena for my early afternoon departure for Vietnam. The same sergeant who had witnessed my arrival the night before was there and we became engrossed in conversation. When it was time to depart, I started to reach for the two seabags he had been watching for me, but he told me to wait. Two lance corporals were nearby, mopping the floor, and he called them over, telling them to carry the seabags to the plane for me.

Their eyes immediately went to my one stripe and one of them shot back, "He's only a PFC. He can carry his own goddamn seabags!"

The sergeant assumed his command posture and in a firm voice said, "You will carry this PFC's bags to that plane."

With visible irritation and much under the breath muttering, they followed his order. He winked at me, I said goodbye and headed for the plane.

CHAPTER FOUR

It was the middle of the night again when we started our descent into Da Nang. I had flown into many a large city on a commercial airline before and was used to a normal, slow decline with the lights of the city providing illumination. But this descent was sudden, steep, and into pitch blackness. (I later learned this was called the Saigon Landing Technique.) We hit the runway in a hurry and came to rest in front of a large tin building. The Marine Corps made a habit of doing this to me, dropping me off in a strange place in the middle of night. I had arrived at Parris Island in the middle of the night. Nighttime always intensifies your first impression of a new place and the first thing to hit me was the heat, then smells I had never experienced before and not pleasant ones.

A sergeant from CIB met me and we placed my seabags in the back of a jeep. The colonel was off in a different direction and I did not see him but once again until I got back home. The sergeant started the jeep and we sped off into the night, twisting down dirt streets and passing sandbagged bunkers. The sound of gunfire echoed in the thick night air. Explosions of intense light came and went from parachute flares popping overhead as earlier ones faded into the dark horizon, illuminating the bunkers and their sentries standing frozen in their defense position until darkness covered them again.

We pulled into a U-shaped complex of narrow, whitewashed buildings overlooking the Da Nang River. The base of the "U" paralleled the river and had a T-shaped dock protruding out into the water that was dancing with the reflection of the continuous rain of drifting flares on the far bank of the river. The shooting was louder here than at the airfield but nobody seemed unduly concerned about it. I sat in that small building, the nightwatch around me, with the only visible sign of defense snarls of barbed wire winding their way into the black depths of the river. I continued watching the fireworks until dawn — flares, small arms fire and intermittent automatic weapon fire, with tracers showing the direction of their flight through blackness.

To think, just two days earlier I had been having breakfast at home with my wife and children. Now I was sitting on an olive drab folding chair in a room feebly lit by a bare lightbulb hanging from the ceiling. The night breeze coming in through the screen carried the sounds and smells of war.

I know every young man's arrival in Vietnam was a private,

individual experience and that he had to deal with it alone. This was really driven home just recently when I listened to an interview with a friend of mine, John Baines, on the radio. He had commissioned me to do the Vietnam War Memorial for San Antonio, Texas, and he was raising funds for the project. He was asked if he remembered his first impression of Vietnam, and he answered that he not only remembered it but thought of it every day. He had just spent forty hours on a C-130 from the States, with one brief stop in the Philippines. The plane entered the air space over Vietnam at 1:30 in the morning and, twenty minutes before it was due to land, an Air Force sergeant stood up and announced, "Lock and load, gentlemen. Quang Tri is at present under siege. When we touch down, we will roll to the end of the runway and turn immediately, simultaneously dropping the ramp. We will not stop. You will depart on the double and find the nearest cover."

The descent was steep, the noise from the engines drowning the outside sounds of battle. As the turn-around began at the end of the runway, the ramp dropped, exposing the sounds and smells of battle raging outside. The men leapt to the runway and headed off into the darkness and the first available cover. My friend found a shellhole to enter, then turned to watch the plane lift back up into the dark sky and safety.

The second plane was right behind, coming in to deposit its load of men. The runway had since taken several rounds of mortars, leaving some craters, and as he watched the C-130 racing for the turn-around, one of its wheels made contact with a crater. Suddenly the wing dipped, then the propeller hit the runway and came off its mounting. It cartwheeled back through the fusilage, opening it like a giant can opener. The plane erupted into a ball of fire, framing the violent, tragic end of its fleeing passengers, themselves engulfed in flames.

This happened during my friend's first twenty minutes in Vietnam but he was still in shock from it when he went back home, and it was a vision that time has done little to soften.

This was a major difference that set the Vietnam War apart from earlier wars in which our country was involved. There was no long boat ride, no long stays in staging areas in a foreign country before embarking for a battle zone. Most Vietnam-bound men were exposed to combat conditions within forty-eight hours of their departures from the States.

CIB was a small unit located across the river from III MAF

Headquarters, Da Nang. It consisted of about thirty Marines who were combat writers, photographers, sound recorders, and an escort service for the news media. There were four sergeants directly assigned to that latter duty and they drew from the lower ranks of other assignments if they needed an extra hand to assist them in their duties. They told me the permanent whitewashed structure in the compound was an old French whorehouse before they took over its occupancy.

I settled in during the next few days and got to know who was who — or thought I did. I was there more than two months before I realized the man who changed our money into piasters, handed out the military scrip on payday, and ran the enlisted men's club as well as the officers' bar was a Marine master sergeant. I hadn't recognized the uniform: a flowered Hawaiian shirt and a forever-present cigar protruding from the corner of his mouth as he talked. We had a Colonel who was obviously being kept out of anything serious for the protection of the Marine Corps. We had a Major who wore wings on his chest but was assigned to desk duty here. Other officers passed in and out. One I talked to was on temporary active duty because he was on the run from his ex-wife. We had an Englishman, Sergeant Livingston, who had initially gone to Canada from England to join their Army in hopes of getting to Vietnam; when that didn't work, he accomplished his goal by coming to the States and joining the Marine Corps. Staff Sergeants Green, Knight, and Shaad were the other assigned escorts for the press.

Lieutenant Len Dermontt was my studio mate. He was very nice to me and had a lot of talent in watercolors. He had attended an art school in the east and done some understudy work with another artist. He had been an artillery officer at Camp Carroll when the opportunity came up for this new program and moved him to Da Nang CIB.

Corporal Ferrara was one of the more colorful young photographers in the compound. He had one of those aggressive, funny personalities you couldn't help but like, and General Walt liked him a lot. Back at Camp Lejune, he had been a machine gunner about ready to be shipped out to Vietnam with his unit. One day, a sergeant asked for volunteers to go to Washington, D.C., for training as combat photographers. No hands were raised so, to his dismay, Ferrara was picked. He was very depressed because he had wanted to be a fighting Marine; this was like being shipped from the football team to the band. But fate

took over and, to his surprise, he was involved in more combat than if he had stayed with his old unit. By the time I got there, he had been in more than ten major operations, been wounded twice, and had spent a month in Japan recovering from his last wound.

We had another combat photographer I thought was carrying an extra burden, being Oriental. His name was Sergeant Lee. In our job, we would join units in the field in the process of an operation. They were not familiar with us and we were not part of their squads or fire teams. I could imagine Sergeant Lee during a nighttime fire fight being next to a Marine who didn't know him and who, if an illumination flare lit up that Oriental face, might very easily over-react.

Once Sergeant Lee was on patrol with a small group of Marines outside Da Nang when they made contact with a large group of VC. As the fire fight progressed, Lee was going about his business, taking photographs of the action, when he felt a sudden tug on his pant leg. Looking down, he saw a young, wounded Marine who weakly informed him that he, Sergeant Lee, was the highest ranking Marine left alive and that the VC had left their cover and were coming across the rice paddy for the final kill. Sergeant Lee immediately traded his camera for a radio, stood up under hostile fire, and directed and corrected the artillery fire on the advancing enemy, stopping their progress and saving those still alive. He received a Bronze Star for his actions.

Our unit was small and well exposed to the perils of war. Its members had their share of record book acknowledgements. Sergeant Shaad and I became friends and he took me under his wing, which I definitely needed. He showed me the ropes on how to get around, and when we were in trouble he'd point where I should head. He had been a drill instructor at Parris Island for two years and had also been a troop handler at Quantico, Virginia, for the Marine Corps Officers Candidate School. Sergeant Shaad was quite a Marine's Marine, right off the poster.

LOCAL ART CRITIC

CHAPTER FIVE

I was like a greenhorn in the Old West and very susceptible to making mistakes. I made several after I accepted an invitation from a sergeant to drive with him and another sergeant to the small village of Hoi An located out of Da Nang. He wanted to trade a radio to a Vietnamese policeman for his .38 revolver. Off we went on my first excursion through the countryside.

I sat in the back of the jeep, taking it all in with great interest. One of the first things that struck me was how life went on in the midst of war. People worked in the fields while billows of smoke rising from the tree line behind them marked the explosions of bombs and artillery shells in the nearby jungle. Women and men strained hard under heavy loads balanced on each end of a stick, using their shoulders as fulcrums. They reminded me of Justice, balancing her scales instead of vegetables. Men and boys followed behind their water buffaloes, splashing through the muddy water in their bare feet. I had thought that the massive effort of the war would have brought the normal pace of the country to a standstill.

The countryside we sped through was visually beautiful. I was seeing scenes I'd only seen before painted on Oriental screens in antique shops or Chinese restaurants back home: men and women standing in water with their pants rolled up, cone-shaped hats shielding their faces from the sun; men standing at the rear of long, narrow boats, poling their way to their destinations.

We passed Marble Mountain, rising abruptly from its reflection in the flat rice paddies spread before it, the sharp, jagged edges of its peaks tearing at the tranquility of the sky above. It was like a giant black dragon rising out of the water, an illusion straight out of some Oriental legend. All this beauty was constantly surrounded by the sounds of war, breaking its visual serenity.

The sergeant drove steadily on, showing no concern for the sights or sounds around us. We stopped at a CAC unit located just outside Hoi An. A CAC unit is small, made up of twelve Marines and one Navy corpsman, and the abbreviation stands for Combined Action Corps. Each unit occupied some sort of permanent structure located near a small village in the countryside. All permanent structures had previously been abandoned by the local villagers. If they had continued staying in the buildings, they would have been considered pro-government politically, and easy targets for the VC due to their lack

of everyday protection in this rural location. Outside major cities, use of any kind of permanent structure was avoided except by government troops or police.

These particular villagers were right in the middle between the VC and the South Vietnamese government, and both exploited them for men and food. Our troops tried to keep both off the backs of the local people and this was probably the most successful pacification program we had going for us in the rural areas.

The young Marines had gained the confidence of the villagers just through their youth and the fact that they stayed on day after day, befriending them — usually the kids first, then the mama-sans. Mothers are mothers all over the world and these couldn't resist the young boys sitting on their sandbags, handing out cokes and candy to the kids. The village men took longer to give in to friendship. But as the Marines helped the villagers by taking care of basic first-aid and even working in the fields at harvest time, the local men began to let them store and protect their harvest. Through this friendship, the villagers also began to supply knowledge of VC movements in the area, and an equal number of men from the village would join the three Marines who left on patrol every three hours, checking the surrounding area for signs of the VC.

In all the villages I visited, there was a definite bond between the local inhabitants and our men — two such different cultures brought together by a situation neither could control. There were no politics involved and with continuous contact, their relationship, like groundwater, sought its own level and showed their value as people to each other.

The brass was not particularly thrilled by these CAC units because their military sharpness became dull after months of more civilian-like existence, making them an easier target for a successful attack by the VC who waited patiently for just the right time.

At CAC, we picked up a young Marine to take us into the village to find the policeman for the trade. He climbed into our jeep, his rifle and heavy cartridge belt held up by suspender straps from one of which a grenade was hanging. As we neared the outskirts of the village, he pointed to a grass "hooch" we were to stop in front of so he could go in and get the necessary information to complete the sergeant's trade. He sprang from the jeep, hitting the ground on a run toward the hut, and in

his haste he didn't notice that his grenade hit the ground and lay beside the jeep in the dirt road.

In an instinctive, naive reaction, I said, "I'll get it!"

I started for it, but a hand grabbed the back of my shirt and jerked me down on the opposite side of the jeep, putting it between us and the grenade.

A stern sergeant's voice said, "Let's wait here a minute!"

Then the enormity of my ignorance hit, and a vision filled my head of my wife getting a telegram stating: "Disregarding his personal safety and for the protection of others, he threw himself on a live grenade." Fortunately, the pin stayed in and the spoon didn't fly, so my foolish mistake wasn't accentuated by a bang. We all got back into the jeep, me feeling very stupid. The young Marine returned, unaware of what had happened until we handed back his grenade.

We followed his directions into the village where a Vietnamese policeman was pointed out to us. We approached him in the jeep and the other sergeant and I stayed in the vehicle as the sergeant and his guide went forward on foot. In looking around, I became nervous, realizing we were the only visible American troops here. This was my first field trip, so to speak, and obviously I didn't know the rules. I had just heard plenty of stories. I knew the enemy didn't have numbers on their backs and I definitely didn't have a program. As we sat there, an old man on a bike pedaled right up and stopped at the jeep, resting his foot on the well and smiling at us without saying anything. He had a brown paper sack with him so I started to slide my hand back to the Browning 9mm pistol at my side.

The sergeant in the jeep with me noticed this and said, smiling sarcastically, "He's okay. They have to have black pajamas on."

Then, out of the corner of my eye, I observed three Vietnamese coming toward us between the hut and our jeep. I was sure this was it and started to react, but again the sergeant grabbed my arm and said, "They got to have guns," still smiling.

This was becoming nerve-wracking and I wanted to move on.

The sergeant completed his trade and we dropped the Marine back at his CAC unit and headed back toward Da Nang. As we drove down the narrow, bumpy dirt road, dust flying up behind us to mark our progress, we came to an abrupt stop behind a bus that was loading. Due to the narrowness of the road we couldn't get around it easily, so we sat there watching the rearrangement of people, ducks, pigs, and over-sized bundles that

was necessary to get everybody aboard. They were hanging out the windows and off the sides of the roof, making the vehicle look like a comical Noah's Ark on wheels. All of a sudden there was a sharp crack.

I said, "Is that what I think it is?"

"Yup," said the sergeant.

He pushed the accelerator to the floor, we squeezed by the bus with much bouncing and flying dust, and raced out of range of our would-be assassin, making our day but not his.

Everything was so different and out of the context I had expected, with moods and feelings fluctuating so fast. It all looked like civilians living and working normally in the middle of giant, unorganized military maneuvers. When I got back to CIB, I realized I'd better get my act together before I hurt myself or got somebody else hurt through my stupidity. Sergeant Shaad and I had a natural rapport and I attached myself to him to try to keep myself alive by learning the rules of survival from the best, which he was.

CA-C D6; Hoi An

31

We received word that something was shaping up near Khe Sanh so Sergeant Shaad and I caught a C-130 in Da Nang and headed in that direction. This was my first trip to the bush and I had no knowledge or sense of what was before me. As we dropped out of the sky on Khe Sanh, I looked out the little porthole window. There was this wisp of a waterfall dropping gently away from the end of the runway we were approaching. It looked like a picture postcard as it made contact with the lush green valley below. As we touched down and rolled to a stop, what had been easy chatter between the men stopped and I didn't know why.

When the ramp at the rear of the plane dropped, a smell new to me permeated the air. Shaad drew up in military stance and left the plane in silence. I stepped from the plane also and started off across the runway behind him. As I walked along I saw, for the first time, the true effects of war. Several Marines were carrying a green bag between them and another Marine was following along with a leg in his hand. Others were lifting wounded off landing choppers, laying them to rest on the runway to determine the order of their needs.

There were civilian reporters aboard our C-130, one of them being Cathy Leroy who was to become famous in photographing the events of the next few days. There were also some other reporters from UPI, but Cathy, being a woman, stood out, of course. She was very small, maybe 110 pounds. I overheard her answer a question put by one of the other reporters as to what she was doing there.

Her reply was, "Oh, I'm just going out to watch the big, bad Marines get dinged."

I was taken aback by her statement and the coldness of her sarcasm. I didn't know at the time that she was French and leaned toward an anti-American view of our involvement in the war her country had lost, along with control of Vietnam. Their last big battle had been in this very area.

We approached the CIB tent and a Marine gunnery sergeant came out to brief the reporters on what was taking place that moment in the nearby hills. One very smartly dressed reporter named Adam Raphael, wearing a freshly pressed jungle safari shirt, was standing there with his camera crew. He pressed forward toward the sergeant, who was Hawaiian, a bit nervous, and obviously had no great command of the King's English. Adam became very impatient with the sergeant's slow explana-

tion of the situation. Instead of listening, he took a superior attitude and started putting words in the sergeant's mouth.

The sergeant kept saying, "That's not what I said."

Adam would say, "You mean it's over?"

"No, I said we may have pulled back to assess the strength of the enemy forces."

Adam finally stomped off and caught the next C-130 out of there. Of course, the action heated up and turned out to be one of the biggest battles of the war. Through his superior attitude and impatience with someone trying to do his best to advise us accurately of the situation, he missed a big story. Cathy Leroy, on the other hand, became world-famous because of her photographs of the battle which appeared in the pages of *Life* magazine.

Shaad and I went back to the runway, trying to get out on a Medivac chopper that wasn't full of priority supplies. We helped with stretchers until darkness cancelled our efforts for that day. As the black of night fell over Khe Sanh, small shafts of extreme white light escaped from openings in the emergency medical tents as the occupants continued their lifesaving duties. I was standing in the dark, the sound of artillery all around me, looking into the operating room seemingly cut in half by the partially rolled up sides of the tent. I watched the corpsmen and doctors perform their tasks; it was like a fish observing people wading in its pond, the only movement it could see being below the water's surface. As I watched the quick movements of legs and hands at work, I could see the supine wounded Marine completely. The frantic efforts of the corpsmen and doctors to stabilize and save seemed to be reaching in from another world. I watched a Marine laid out on a table before me; there was no time for proper anesthesia and two corpsmen laid their compassionate weight over him to keep him on the table and control his spasms. A calf was missing from one leg and there was a hole in his chest so big three doctors had their hands inside in an effort to help him with his gallant fight for life, a drama witnessed by only a few in this dark, lonely place. Its outcome would send shock waves halfway around the world to his family but this desperate fight for life would never be known by them. Only a young, healthy, perfectly tuned body could fight off untimely destruction with such furious determination.

With first light, Shaad and I were able to get out on a chopper loaded with a news crew to a hill some distance from Hill 881

South. He and I managed to get another helicopter in the field and eventually we stepped off the large, dark green CH-46 onto the grass-covered hill that lay before Hill 881 South. The Marines were just regrouping and had sustained heavy casualties. The mortar teams were busy with their harassing fire. A M-60 machine gun chattered away with a shirtless gunny sergeant standing beside it, binoculars in hand, directing the crew's fire, telling them to shorten the burst, scolding them for not bringing along the second barrel to change when this one got too hot for use.

The rest of the Marines were digging in for the night, their talk sparked by the adrenalin of the events that had just taken place, asking one another if they had seen common friends hit during the fierce fire fight. All of this had started for them six days ago on April 25, at the rugged edge of Khe Sanh.

CHAPTER SEVEN

Mike Company arrived at Khe Sanh on April 25, 1967, and spent the next two nights sleeping on the perimeter. They moved out on the morning of the 28th with other Marine Corps units designated to start this operation which was called Union I (later to be changed to Union II). The objective was to clear off the tops of Hills 881 North and South of the North Vietnamese buildup reported by Marine Intelligence. Don Hossack was part of the 2nd Platoon, Mike Company 3/3, as their radioman on this little trek in the mountainous north part of South Vietnam near the Laotian border.

The day was very warm so it was decided that Mike Company's men should shed their flak jackets for the impending operation. This was done in the hope of relieving some of the heat problems that could possibly bring on heat stroke from the extreme exertion of their journey in this high, rugged country.

They left for the Hills using a well-traveled trail obviously used by the NVA. Lying along both sides of the trail were many square-shaped foxholes with smooth sides which was the technique used by the NVA for building foxholes. When the order came to saddle up and move out again, it would be much easier for him to get to his feet with the radio on his back from the half-sitting position the sides of the foxhole gave him.

His sergeant (as only a sergeant can do!) remarked on the intelligence level his action had just displayed and asked, "Is this condition permanent, stupid?"

He also not so gently reminded Don the foxhole could have been boobytrapped and they would not be having this conversation at this moment. Don never made that mistake again!

The Marines moved on over the winding trail edged by tall sawgrass, step by step drawing closer to their objective, walking until the last visible light from the dying sun sinking in the west had faded. Unable to see the trail any more, 1st Squad of 1st Platoon was sent a little further ahead on the trail to set up a point ambush position for the night. The rest of Mike Company lay down on the trail in single file, each man facing outward in a direction opposite to the man next to him, positioning their packs as temporary pillows. Every other man was awake for two hours of watch, then relieved by his next man who had slept for his two hours. So as not to give away their position in the dark to the enemy who might be lurking in its cover, no talking or cigarettes were allowed. Hundreds of eyes and ears strained to their limits in the silent vigil on this black moonless

Reinforcements-Union II; Khe Sanh

night framed in fear. In such blackness, the sky appeared to be a giant black table top with thousands of sparkling diamonds scattered over its surface. One of the diamonds would now and then fall off the table, leaving a thin, bright trail of light as it fell into eternity.

The slow time of darkness finally broke in the east with the first glow of the coming birth of the new day's sun. As the light intensified, Mike Company's men, moving with morning stiffness in their bones from the hard ground they had slept on, fought the manipulation of C-ration church keys to get at the cold, tasteless breakfast hiding in small green cans. The command given to move out, they lifted their burdens to their backs to continue their slow journey through the never ending sea of grass that rolled like waves in the occasional gust of wind.

Further on that day, Mike Company came across a small stream that had carved its path through the tall grass, its waters racing for some river in the far-off valleys below. It was only twelve inches wide but flowed with clear water. The hot Marines splashed their faces, wiped their arms, and drank the ice cold water. The climb from Khe Sanh was a long, hot, steady pace uphill, and the stream was a welcome surprise to all. As Don filled his canteen from it, he couldn't help but think of similar fast-moving brooks he had drunk from at home in the mountains of Montana.

Later that afternoon, they came to a small hill that lay just before Hill 881 South, their objective looming up before them in plain view. The mountain air at this point was heavy with the odor of death. The smell was very familiar to all the veteran soldiers as to its unmistakable origin, leading them to two bodies lying in the cover of tall, thick grass. There had been a platoon of Marines through here just a week before and they had had a fierce fire fight with the enemy. They had recovered ten bodies from that engagement but had been unable to locate two other Marines and had to list them as missing in action. Today their fate was revealed by the wind carrying the smell of their rotting flesh to the arrival of fresh Marines. They were placed in body bags to be returned the next day to Khe Sanh and home for their final rest. Mike Company's men then let their heavy packs hit the ground and turned to building a night defense position. Don dug an extra hole for his radio to protect it in case of attack that night.

Occupying their night defense positions, straining for vision in the dimming light of day, everyone could sense the closeness of the enemy. As the night gained age, there was suddenly contact made with the enemy. It was verbal contact, the NVA showing their confidence in the coming battle that was no secret now. The Marines at this moment had no reason to know the NVA had ample justification for their confidence.

Their diction incredibly good, the NVA soldiers shouted up at the Marines from the deep ravine that lay between them and Hill 881 South. In clear, precise English, their voices using the night air as a natural amplifying system to achieve the quality of a Sony stereo system, they called, "Marine! Put your helmet on, we are coming to get you!"

The Hill battle had just begun, the first volley of fire a barrage of taunting words. Words have started all wars but today's politicians don't shout them from foxholes to suffer the immediate violent retaliation for them.

The verbal bullets were the only ones fired that night by the enemy. Dawn arrived on time, carrying the morning sounds of grunts and groans of men loading on their backs their assigned heavy gear for this day's assault. It was now the morning of April 30, 1967.

Mike Company headed down into the valley from which had come the enemy's taunts the night before. The sun was blocked now by the dense jungle on the valley floor that lay before Hill 881 South. A wide trail ran through the center and it was impossible to move off of it because of the thickness of the jungle that lined its sides. Don found a small dug hole that had some communication wire leading up to the top of the hill; it was an NVA listening post. They also came across a Russian rifle, left behind no doubt accidentally. Some NVA soldier was definitely getting his ass chewed out by his sergeant for his carelessness. The rifle was unusually long and of heavy caliber with a scope of at least 12-power mounted on it. This was not a weapon known to be in the enemy's arsenal at this time.

Mike Company arrived at the center of the hill and stopped momentarily to adjust equipment, sending a chilling sound of cold steel clanking as hundreds of bayonets were affixed atop ends of their gun barrels. Looking upward, 1st Platoon started the ascent with 2nd Platoon right behind them; 3rd Platoon was held in reserve. The men started up single file and someone fired a Light Anti-Tank Weapon. It had so little range, it only went halfway up the hill and exploded harmlessly, its only effect to announce to the enemy that the Marines were coming up. As they climbed, Don could see the NVA moving around on the top of the hill, not showing any particular panic for what was about to transpire.

The climb was hard and slow; there was plenty of time before they would be in effective range of the enemy's guns. As they reached the halfway point, 1st Platoon started to sweep right with 2nd Platoon sweeping left, both spreading out on line to go over the top. Both platoons were drawing some sniper fire and an occasional grenade. Just enough fire to let the Marines know the NVA was there but not enough to make them stop their advance up the hill. As Don, with 2nd Platoon, moved out onto the summit of the ridge and closed in on the top of the hill, they saw there was more grass and less trees than expected. What trees there were beckoned to the Marines' instinct for cover; nobody yet realized all of this was a well-designed plan.

As the Marines began to move over the top, the point man was the first to go down, shot in the buttocks. Then all Hell broke loose; they had been sucked into a trap of well-aimed crossfire in anticipation of where they would head for cover. The first few moments were devastating to men and equipment as a murderous crossfire and mortars rained down on the stunned Marines. So did bad luck.

The machine gunner jumped to his feet in pure instinctive reaction, ammo belt dragging the ground, firing at the bunker before him. An RPD immediately responded to his action, slamming a round into the machine gun receiver, shattering it, another round tearing away the lower part of the young Marine's face as he went over backwards. Don, four feet away in a bomb crater with his lieutenant, watched as a corporal made a mad dash for the fallen machine gun which was so important in their desperate situation. As he and three other Marines frantically tried to repair it, Don heard his last words.

"I don't think I can fix it, sir," he shouted to the lieutenant. He disintegrated before Don's eyes as a mortar struck him, killing the other three Marines at the same time. The next mortar crashed in and this time Don was the victim. The lieutenant was up on his knees trying to see when suddenly the wooden pump on his shotgun shattered from the impact of a bullet, sending splinters into the lieutenant's face. He turned to Don with small pieces of wood protruding from his face.

With amazement and shock in his voice, he said, "Did you see

that?", then turned back to the direction in which he had been looking.

Don was adjusting the battle dressing he was putting on his wound; finally, it was fixed! He turned back to find just above his head the lieutenant's boots, jerking with the last bit of the lieutenant's life. Don pulled him back into the hole and turned him over, saying, "Oh, shit, he's going to die," expecting a big hole somewhere. There was none; only a small pinhole in his cheekbone marking the entrance where a small piece of shrapnel had entered. Apparently, it had been deflected into the brain, killing the lieutenant.

Another corporal nearby became disoriented and started shouting irrationally when the violent death of the Marine next to him left his face splattered with the dead Marine's brains.

The battle wasn't even twenty minutes old and already Don was surrounded by dead, his lieutenant also killed. He got off a fast message to the other platoon in code, saying "Kangaroo," which meant his platoon had already suffered dead in the initial contact with the enemy. Then hearing cries for a medic from nearby, Don crawled toward the sound and found the wounded man. He turned the Marine over but it was useless — death was but moments away.

The M79 man had been shot in the ankle, leaving the foot attached by only a small piece of skin, adding to the loss of valuable fire power that was crumbling all around him. The new M-16's were jamming on the Marines who were trying desperately to fight back with some effect against the enemy's fire power that was cutting them to ribbons.

Don was calling 1st Platoon on the radio to make sure they didn't fire in 2nd Platoon's direction. The 1st was also under heavy attack and as Don was talking to their radio operator, he was cut off in mid-sentence as the other's radio went silent. The radio operator wore glasses and apparently the lenses had caught the sun just right, exposing his position to that new Russian rifle in an NVA sniper's hand. He was shot through the eye and killed instantly. Don did manage to talk to the lieutenant who grabbed the handset from the dead Marine's hand.

Those Marines on the front line were firing in between fixing the jamming of the M-16's and screaming for more ammo and cleaning rods to help with the rifle's malfunction. Don now had another Marine in the hole with him and the two of them crawled out of the hole and began stripping the dead of ammo

and cleaning rods. They pitched the ammo and rods forward to the Marines in front of them who were pinned down but still fighting desperately. On Don's request for more ammo, he came across his best friend in the platoon who was seriously wounded. While Don tried to stop the bleeding and apply a battle dressing, at the same time holding and reassuring him, he died in Don's arms. In sadness, Don remembered how his friend had talked often of becoming a Baptist minister after he got out of the Marine Corps.

Leaving his friend's body lying on the dark red dirt of this tragic hill, his soul lifted from it by death's black hand, Don and the other Marine crawled back into the hole with the radio. Don tried to go up to Air Tac on the radio to make contact with the gunships laying off about two klicks from their position. Just as he was attempting this, they both heard the pop and fizzle of an NVA grenade as it came into the hole with them. The other Marine rolled out of the hole in time but Don, stiffening from his wound, was not as fast in his exit. The soft dirt of the bomb crater absorbed a lot of the explosion but not enough. Don found himself wounded again.

With men and equipment going down so fast, the Marines could not get their air panels out to mark their position. The gunships had to hold back, putting them and many others watching this action in a very powerless and thus frustrating situation as Mike Company was being made into hamburger.

Don, wounded twice but still trying to do his job, raised up for a better view and to see if anybody had gotten the air panels out. A piece of shrapnel slammed through the front of his helmet. Thin, about five inches long, it came to rest at the back of his helmet, burning the back of his head. With his head feeling as if it had been stuck into a beehive, he frantically tore the helmet off, flinging it to the ground. Bells were ringing in his ears; he shook his head to try to clear it and found he was hearing whistles also. In a few moments, the bells subsided but he kept hearing the whistles. Then it hit him: The NVA was maneuvering to overrun them. Remembering 3rd Platoon in reserve, he grabbed the radio and called for reinforcements.

Still dazed from his wounds which were beginning to really hurt, Don looked up from the bottom of the hold to check the results of his phone call. Two staff sergeants were standing on the edge of the hole. Don handed them the radio, telling them at the same time to get down. One said, "Boy! You're a mess!

You'd better work your way back to the center of the hill and down."

They turned and disappeared with the twelve additional men they had brought with them to try to turn the tide of the battle. Their efforts ended shortly in their deaths. It was now obvious all was lost.

A sergeant from Don's platoon had fought his way into an NVA bunker and dragged six seriously wounded Marines in with him. He had a radio and, seeing the hopeless siutation, he called in Willie Peter artillery to cover the top of the hill in smoke for the retreat now in progress. He dragged the six wounded Marines from the bunker to safety under heavy fire. (He later received the Silver Star for his lifesaving actions in this battle.)

Don had caught up with a Marine less wounded than he and they leaned on each other as they headed for the bottom of the hill. The many dead had to be left behind; priority had to be given to the wounded during the retreat. The wounded were dragged, rolled, and pushed down the steep, bloodstained hill, all under NVA fire.

Don crossed the valley and found a large bomb crater with three other wounded Marines from Mike Company. Quiet conversation passed between the stunned men who thought they were at last safe from the enemy bullets. As Don talked to a squad leader across from him who had been shot in the chest, he noticed fresh blood running down the man's leg and advised him he should put a battle dressing on it. The young Marine could not believe he had just been shot again from across the valley. It seemed like an impossible distance but that Russian rifle had struck again as it had so often that day, delivering its accurate stroke of death to the pinned-down Marines one at a time.

Don had lived his nightmare for four hours. By ten o'clock that night, he landed on the hospital ship "Repose" to start the nightmares for the rest of his life from this day's events.

Mike Company ceased to exist on this day; out of 190 men only 26 were left standing. All others were either dead or wounded in their effort and sacrifice to uphold the highest tradition of Marine Corps history. These Hills 881 South and 881 North, which were side by side and where the fighting was taking place simultaneously, were eventually to kill over 350 Marines and wound more than 1,000 before their battles ended.

49

Shaad and I set about picking our foxhole site for the on-coming night. My faith in Dick always increased in moments like this so I jokingly made a deal with him: I would dig the hole if he would stay with me for the night. But of course, he helped — it takes a big hole to sink this over six-foot post in the ground. The sounds of battle were dying off except for a few bursts of fire to let the enemy know we hadn't gone home. Once in awhile, over the sounds of choppers scurrying here and there and outgoing mortars, a voice of authority would remind everyone not to bunch up. Shaad and I sat near our hole as night covered us like a blanket. This was my first night in combat and the dark really intensifies sounds and smells — even more, it intensifies fear.

It all seemed like a dream as we sat there in the dirt and tall grass, our faces fading in and out as one illumination flare died a natural death hanging from its gently falling parachute only to be replaced by the intense light of the next. Salvos of artillery announced their departure from far-off Khe Sanh in a soft drum-roll of sound; drawing closer to us, their screaming split the night air as they raced their way to a landing, it was hoped, on the hill that lay before us.

We had both graduated from high school in 1957, and this was the month for our tenth anniversary reunions; his was this very night and mine was scheduled for later in the month. We talked of how surprised our classmates would be to learn the reason why we couldn't attend the reunions. I was particularly certain that mine would be since I graduated from a Quaker school in New Town, Pennsylvania.

We talked between salvos, pausing as they passed over us to make sure their course was true. In the midst of all this, "Puff, the Magic Dragon" showed up. This was a plane equipped with electronic mini-cannons that put forth an incredible amount of fire power aimed at targets below. The pilot made a few passes over the hill in front of us, spitting forth his deadly fire at the enemy below. It reminded me

Breakfast operation Hickory
May 1967 Austin Deuel

50

Returning Fire 51

of the fire fall I had seen at Yosemite Park in California.

Dawn finally broke without serious incident and, as it gave way to morning, activity increased as did the sounds of war. First to appear on the scene were the propeller-driven planes of the South Vietnamese Air Force to start the softening up for the imminent assault. In comparison to the faster jets, they always looked as if they had to be pushed from the sky to reach the bottom of their dives. Then the jets showed up, screaming in overhead, releasing their loads of bombs on top of the hill we were about to climb. Large and small pieces of hot, spinning steel thudded down around us, sinking into the soft dirt to end their flight. A Marine near me was struck but not seriously hurt as his bulky equipment took the brunt of the hit; the piece of hot metal fell at his feet and another Marine tried to get him to keep it for luck. Others were not so lucky.

As we waited for the command to move forward, a jet went screaming back up to the safety of the heavens, leaving behind it a tremendous explosion just in front of us. I looked up to see a large tree trunk, twisting and turning in its flight toward our position like a slow-motion movie.

A sergeant near me shouted, "You shittin' me? A thousand yard log throw!", as it passed over our heads and landed behind us with a deafening crash.

A 106 near us started its duty, shooting a 50-caliber tracer until it hit the target it sought, then following with the 106 artillery round, the large brass casings building up on the ground as it continued firing.

We started off wearing no flak jackets or packs due to the extreme climb ahead of us. When we reached the valley before the hill, we stopped to organize for the assault. Now, with every report of the 106, shrapnel rained down on us, sounding like the first heavy drops of a summer rainstorm as it came through the foliage. We formed three single files about a hundred yards apart, and as the first Marine started up from my section, I fell in behind him. The summit was out of sight, the tempo very slow, giving me a false sense of my physical ability to make this climb. The tempo never changed but I began having difficulty with it as we drew closer to the top. I remembered that I had bragged to Shaad the night before that the Marine Corps had never once pushed me to my physical limits. Well, the gods were getting even with me now! I was in trouble. I hung in there only because of the fear that if I stopped to catch my

Support Fire; Hill 881 South   53

breath the Marine in front of me might be hung out to dry if he made contact with the enemy and I held up his support with my inability to go on. My physical condition had been pushed to its limit as we closed in on the ridge of the summit. My insides were screaming with pain, the smell of death became overpowering, and we could see how much punishment by bomb and shell had been taken by the ground and trees. As we passed over the edge of the summit, I came face to face with man's insanity at its outermost limits.

Shaad sat next to me in silence as I threw up and fought off shock. I finally gained my composure and started to walk around. It was a hell of a fight. Most of the dead were lying on the edge of the ridge. Some had been tended to by corpsmen and, still living, dragged to the bases of shot-off trees for protection from the murderous crossfire, but to no avail. There had been openings close by, unseen from the large bunker complex that was on top of the hill, allowing the enemy to emerge near and finish off the wounded where they lay. The bunker complex was extensive; there were a few places exposed by direct bomb hits and the logs that were jutting upward were each a foot in diameter, giving a clue to the massive size of the bunker lying underneath the ground. One young Marine had made it to a slit trench that connected to a bunker opening. He had to have crossed an exposed field of deadly fire. His feet were in the trench but his upper body lay bent back out from the force of his death. His effort must have been beyond description and it was obvious to me that uncommon valor was a common occurrence here.

Only Marines lay dead; not one enemy body was found, only their shattered sandals, pieces of their weapons, a stretcher or two with splintered bamboo poles. Our dead still had their weapons in hand, showing the contempt the enemy had for the newly issued M-16, an opinion the Marines also held. Its unreliable function had contributed as much as enemy bullets to this tragic carnage.

The scene before me brought thoughts of past wars. The uniforms were different and so were the causes, like Custer's last stand and Wounded Knee, but the settings are always the same: the grotesque sight of naked death. The dates are different but it's apparent we never learn from our past.

Some of our men began to set up a perimeter defense and check out the external parts of the bunkers; other Marines

started to collect the dead. I helped one Marine as he tried to place a fallen comrade in a body bag. His rigid arms were frozen in their reach for the sky and, as I tightened my grip, my thumb went right through the tight, crisp skin. I had to place my soft utility cap in my hand so as to not repeat this desecration as we continued our efforts. We finally achieved our purpose and placed him with the increasing line of bags. The silence of death was only broken by Marines asking one another, "Did you see where Bill got it?" or "Have you found Jerry yet?"

As the search for lost comrades continued, the sky became very dark and the wind picked up as a thunderstorm left a nearby hill, crossed the valley between and headed in our direction. The rain was cold and we started taking ponchos from the packs of the dead.

An officer screamed in frustration, "The next Marine that takes a poncho from the dead will be court-martialed!"

The water, puddling up, reflected the remains of shell-shattered trees in mirror-like surfaces framed in red dirt that darkened as it became wetter. The wind was fierce now, with increased flashes of lightning followed by the thunder of the Lord's cannon. The landscape had the stark, hunted look of pictures I had seen of World War I.

Shaad and I were in a bomb crater with another Marine, watching in silence as the water got deeper around our feet. There was a tremendous lightning flash, three more Marines went down, and a cry for "Medic!" lifted above the sounds of the storm. This was the last straw for the young Marine next to me. Uncontrollably, he blurted out in a soft, desperate voice, "Even God is against us."

The storm passed over shortly, leaving us wet and cold and with more casualties to contend with. When we had finished finding all the dead, the choppers came in to lift them out. As soon as there was room, Shaad and I left to go back to Khe Sanh. I was numb from my experience. As I stepped from the chopper at Khe Sanh, Sergeants Green and Knight were there from Da Nang. They had thought I'd been hit since my pack showed up without me; they didn't know we had shed our equipment for the climb up Hill 881 South.

Shaad and I helped unload another group of incoming wounded from choppers and the next thing I remember was sitting in a C-130, gazing blankly out the open back end as they finished loading it. I realized I was becoming unusually attractive

57

to a growing number of flies. Not resisting their attention, I
looked down at my arms and saw they were covered
with drying blood. The rear door raised slowly, closing
the curtain on one of life's dramas that should never have
happened. The pilot, standing on his brakes, revved up the
engines until they sounded as if they were going to leave without
us. Then he released the brakes and we raced for the heavens, passing over
that gentle wisp of waterfall, so innocent and soft-looking as it disappeared from
beneath us, hiding the signs of the life-and-death struggle that went on
around it daily.

60 *Even God Is Against Us- preceding page*

I returned to CIB and the art studio I shared with Lieutenant Dermontt in Da Nang. Corporal Ferrara taught me how to develop my own film and I got back into the routine of painting. It was back to Batman movies and beer in the enlisted men's club. To break my routine, I helped with the chore of filling sandbags to protect our generator and other key positions. It was a good opportunity to get to know the local kids who hung around in swarms, wanting to help in return for any kind of reward. They were so slight in build but would happily struggle with impossible loads. They were all familiar with our western movies and would mimic the cowboys, drawing their hands up sharply with finger extended in pistol fashion and giggling at our attempts to beat their quick draws. They were also fascinated by the unusual amount of hair on my arms and chest. They would reach out shyly to touch and stroke it, pulling their hands back quickly at first until they gained confidence; then they'd try to pull it out.

An event took place several days after I returned to CIB that would change my attitude toward the leadership of our country and its war generals. It has left me with a lifetime of distrust of their word in any event unless I've seen it with my own eyes.

I attended a press conference General Walt held at CIB about Hills 881 South and North. The press had gotten hold of information about the performance of the M-16 and was creating a lot of flak — I must say rightly so. I stood there as the general explained to the news people what had transpired. He blamed the rifle's poor performance on poor field maintenance by the troops. Nothing could have been further from the truth. Most of the Marines on those hills were veterans of at least nine months in Vietnam and had proven reason to be skeptical of the weapon long before the battle of Hills 881 South and North. I watched them work on it constantly. They carried paint brushes in their helmets and wrote home asking their folks to send them WD40 because the dry lubricant issued with the weapon by the Government wasn't any good. In the field I constantly heard the request for a test fire as they worked on the weapons, trying to fix the persistent problem.

The jamming that occurred was the worst kind to try to clear in a hurry. A new round was stripped in on top of a round that had failed to be extracted from the chamber after firing, so you had to pry the new round out, then hand-extract the round stuck in the chamber. Once cleared, the jamming would usually

happen again very shortly. The Marines in the field felt it was an extractor problem because some of the rifles were good and others were plagued with the problem continually. They felt the chambers were off on their milling which increased the poundage the extractor needed to complete its job; this was too much for it, so it would just skip over that one and trip in a new round on top of it.

The general had an ordnance major enumerate the advantages of the M-16 if properly cared for, and some of the nomenclature and its rate of fire and so forth. I couldn't believe the blame for this tragedy being so unfairly misdirected to its victims. It was the same as blaming the passengers on the "Titanic" for buying a ticket and thus causing their unfortunate accident. I know that later on they blamed bad powder for the problem but at any rate, they did eventually change the design. In the existing rifles, they changed every one of the bolts to an improved version and eliminated the extraction problem. Though the problem was well known before this sad event, it took a tragedy such as this to speed up acknowledgement of its severity and institute correction.

It was obvious the leaders, including the President, were taking care of their own public images. I know every war has its incompetents who seek the limelight at the expense of life and limb of others, but this war was infested with them beyond any normal proportion. The truth was manipulated for careers and power, or even out of fear that careers would end abruptly for being on the wrong team. These people used our innocent youth, with their beliefs in honor and duty to their country and the righteousness of that country's purpose in Vietnam.

After the news conference, a wave of depression washed over me. I went back to the studio, wracking my brain over all of this insanity. Then numbness set in; I wanted to go home.

I continued to observe the war differently from that day forward. I had come to Vietnam with very hawkish views. But my opinion of war was that if it were to solve a problem, its purpose should be black and white, not the gray of all this horror created for millions of people on both sides. At Pearl Harbor, we were bombed on a definite day and there was definite loss of lives and property. South Koreans were nearly driven into the sea because of a direct invasion by the North Korean Army, not by guerrilla warfare raging inside their borders, and the territory regained with our help remains intact today. We were

involved in Vietnam over a debate as to whether we were really fired on in the Tonkin Gulf, an incident still suspect at the credibility level since there was only a glow in the dark and some dots on a radar screen. No one even saw the splash of a missile or shell. And here we were losing thousands and killing thousands more. I felt there were two sets of rules: one for those dying and another for those in charge of this fatal destiny.

I walked around CIB trying not to think, to get back to the observation which was my purpose and which I owed the guys. I wasn't sleeping very well and one night I was up late when I heard a commotion. I went outside to investigate and found that a sergeant had surprised three young boys inside our compound, stealing. They dashed for the river and one boy was scooped up by the sergeant as the other two dove in. He managed to hit one of the boys with a rock but the other boy grabbed him and swam out of sight around the barbed wire that twisted into the river. The sergeant placed his one prisoner inside our command building where the occupants harassed the prisoner by menacingly slamming the bolts home on their M-16's to frighten him, which they accomplished quite well. I knew this was a war in which all people were potentially dangerous, no matter what size, but this was still very hard for me to watch. The boy looked no more than twelve years old. At first light, the Vietnamese police showed up to deal with our prisoner. They were even less delicate in their handling of the boy. They threw him in the back of a jeep and sped off with him bouncing up and down as they seemingly hit every bump in the road to punish him more.

Over the years, I had enjoyed the TV series "M.A.S.H." as anyone in the service does. Every outfit has similar characters; we had only one because our outfit was so small. Our "Frank" was a "bird" colonel called "Dingleberry" instead of "Ferret Face." I slept a lot of times on a picnic table in front of the officers' club next to the Da Nang River. I preferred the fresh night air to the stuffy air of the building where I was supposed to sleep. I was backlit by the lights of the officers' club, lights which gave them a view of the river as it passed by the window of the club. I was lying there asleep one night when I was brought back to wakefulness by a sharp crack, then a second one. I realized I was the target for a sniper somewhere off in the darkness. There were two more shots but I was on my way by then, heading for a low rock wall and screaming for someone

to turn off the lights. There was a great flurry of activity because it was highly unusual for us to come under deliberate fire. The colonel appeared in his brilliant white boxer shorts, shower shoes snapping, dogtags flying, a .45 at the ready — altogether a true picture of command. After he determined it wasn't a major probe by the North Vietnamese Army, he returned to his quarters, shower shoes still a-flapping.

General Walt had a personal launch that used to pass by our area often. We of lesser rank knew the crew of the launch and often got rides along with tales of how they used it when the general was out of town. All they had to do was unfurl the general's two star flag and nobody would bother them on their joyrides. One day the launch was coming up the middle of the river, more than 200 yards offshore. The colonel was sitting at his desk in the command building, the screen sides giving him a clear view of the launch's progress as it came up the river from III MAF, its flags wiggling those two stars in the breeze. He watched intently until the launch was about even with the command building, then raced out of the building and down to the T-shaped dock that protruded into the river. Upon reaching the top of the "T", he drew to attention and gave a hand salute as the launch passed. Those of us watching knew the general probably wasn't even on board, and if he was and saw the colonel standing there saluting, he'd probably be wondering who that asshole was.

CHAPTER TEN

I managed to arrange a three-day trip to Saigon by doing a painting for Sergeant Huff who assured me he could obtain proper orders. This was the same sergeant who invited me on my adventure to Hoi An and how he was able to acquire travel orders to Saigon for two Marines I have no idea. At that time, Marines were not allowed in-country liberty at all, so I assume the orders read that our actions would be in some kind of official capacity.

We boarded a C-130, headed south and landed at Tansonahut Air Base about nine o'clock at night. All my Marine experiences seemed scheduled for nighttime introduction, no matter when I set out for them. As we left the plane, Huff had a particular hotel in mind even though he had never been to Saigon before. One of the civilian correspondents at CIB had recommended it to him as being a place for all the good action. Another one of those rumored fishing holes — I'd been on that kind of trip before!

We went into the terminal and did our thing with our orders. I was expecting a protest over their validity but it never came. As we passed through the terminal on our way to find a cab for Saigon, I noticed that the atmosphere was the same as it is at night in all military terminals: the intense light in vivid contrast to the blackness outside; men moving about like zombies as they made half-hearted stabs at their assigned tasks; the air heavy with the smell of diesel fuel. To this day whenever I encounter that smell, my mind's eye returns to the terminals at Kadena, Da Nang, and Saigon.

Huff and I walked out into a night that was black and heavy with humidity, in search of a cab. A small, frail-looking Vietnamese opened the door of his miniature French Renault, inviting us to enter — or perhaps it was a dare, to see if the two of us, each over six feet tall and weighing 200 pounds apiece, could arrange our mass on the tiny back seat and still close the door on what probably seemed to him our oversized human frames. This feat accomplished, he jumped into the front seat next to the driver and we shot off into the darkness as Huff announced the name of the hotel we were seeking. The man who had opened the door was acting as interpreter and tour guide; I'm sure the driver spoke English too, although he never let on that he did. I think they felt safer in pairs and perhaps looked on the operation as somewhat of a game.

Mostly black streaked past the windows but those sights I

Downtown Saigon

71

did see as we neared Saigon reminded me of Da Nang, only bigger. As we penetrated deeper into the city, the buildings became even bigger and Saigon took on the character of a large city. There were still sounds of war about and an occasional glint of flares over the city lights. We sped down narrow streets, taking many quick turns, then coming to a sudden, jerky stop as the guide would turn to us and claim that this was the hotel we were looking for. By now they had figured out that we had never been to Saigon before and hadn't the slightest idea of where we were. At each stop, Huff would stick his head out the window in the direction they were pointing, then proclaim in a frustrated voice, "Noop, this ain't it!" We would then lunge forward through a new web of streets, like a mouse lost in a maze.

At this point we realized they were taking us places where they would get a reward for bringing us there to spend our money. They were well aware that we had no time to switch horses because it was getting close to curfew and this was not a good neighborhood to be walking around in, especially when we didn't know where to head for safety. When curfew was in effect, things moving in dark streets got shot at. They were playing this ace to win their game and we made a final stop at a place where we may well have stopped earlier, its location disguised by their fancy driving. They were probably chuckling over the success of their strategy.

People were scurrying about emptying the sidewalks of bicycles and small motor bikes parked there in great numbers. They placed them inside the establishments where they worked and would have to remain until morning when they would be allowed to move about freely again. This was my first opportunity to witness the effects of martial law on a society and it was strange to observe. Standing on the sidewalk, I stared up at the hotel where we were going to stay and noticed there was no glass in its windows.

Huff was still arguing with our guide about the price of our trip and the guide's inability to get us where we'd asked to go. His final statement was a loudly proclaimed, "No way!", punctuated by his large fist slamming down on the roof of that ill-fated little Renault, leaving its owners a permanent reminder that some games have a price — especially if they're rigged. They made what I'm sure was an on-the-spot business decision and left without further protest.

We entered the hotel bar and proceeded with a typical soldier's night of drinking, loud music, and the attentions of obviously man-starved little ladies who couldn't seem to keep their hands off us. As the night progressed, the girls got prettier, the music got louder, and my dancing ability improved greatly. We were staying on the top floor of the hotel and when we finally got up there about three o'clock in the morning, I went out on the balcony and stared out over this city that was on the news every night all over the world. The city that lay before me was full of life yet seemingly as empty as the middle of nowhere without even a breath of air stirring. This mood was occasionally broken by the low pop of a far-off flare that died silently on the city skyline, and punctuated now and then with a fierce burst of automatic fire that was followed by a bleak silence.

I finally went to bed only to be soon awakened by new daylight. I looked up at the ceiling and took in the sounds of motors, horns, and many people moving about in close quarters; sounds as normal as those of any city in the world as another day of living gathered momentum. Huff and I got up and changed into our civilian clothes for the day's adventures that lay before us. Seeing this new city was like discovering a new painting for me, although I would never tell Huff this — he'd think I was crazy.

We decided that the transportation of the day would be bicycle rickshaws along with our feet. Going through the streets much more slowly than the night before, we passed big buildings with large signs on them in English, labeling familiar and unfamiliar companies from the English-speaking countries. If their size was any indication of their commitment to stay, they looked very permanent to me. The streets also contained native vendors of all classes from the small, entrenched family shops to pushcarts that seemed to be carrying an impossible amount of inventory for their small owners to maneuver through the overcrowded streets.

I have since discovered in my travels through what are considered third world countries that most of them have cities similar to this. See the little boy staring at the sea of people moving past his perch, posed like a kingfisher on a limb over a stream waiting for a fish to come close to the surface. If eye contact is made, the little boy darts into the stream of people, not losing sight of his spotted prey and pushing a box of Juicy Fruit gum forward for a sure sale. His counterpart can be found among the disadvantaged in dozens of cities.

During our self-guided tour of the city, we accidentally found the zoo, which was surrounded by little parks with small, beautiful ponds. Each of these had a tiny island in its center, and at the center of the island was an open air, Oriental style gazebo. A delicate, again Oriental style, bridge skimmed the lily pads and fish to reach the gazebo and it was protected by carved dragons lying at each corner of its roof. Except for these beautiful structures and some Buddhist temples scattered throughout the city, the architecture showed mostly a European influence.

The elephant we saw at the zoo showed the restrictions of martial law, too. He was fastened to a stake by a three-foot chain that restricted his movements to swaying back and forth as he faced the walk and small fence. He swayed in a rhythmic trance that I'm sure he had to maintain to get through his daily ordeal. San Diego Wild Animal Park this was not.

Also in the park area was a bridge across a river that passed slowly beneath its span. The quiet surface of the water was shattered by young boys diving and jumping from the highest point of the bridge. Their laughter at this feat filled the air as they clambered out of the water and up to the top of the bridge for another daring leap. This scene reminded me of myself as a young boy and the bridge I jumped from many times. You put warm water, a bridge, and young boys together and the results are the same all over the world, even in the middle of a war.

Moving on, we passed a large Catholic church, its very Gothic architecture an extreme example of outside influence. Its incongruity was accentuated by young Buddhist monks passing in front of it in their brilliant orange robes. Its sheer size and Gothic shape rising behind them emphasized the simplicity of their existence.

The city did show the effects of war with veterans displaying their war-battered bodies as they begged on street corners along with civilians who had been caught in the war's crossfire. The smells varied as we walked along. Passing restaurants, we could smell their menus; then these savory aromas would be interrupted by blasts of air from alleys and spaces between buildings that carried the smells of filth and decay. There were the usual pockets of the rich in their preferred restaurants, in full sight of the poor people on the street, checking the menu for what they would like to eat while those outside were looking for

anything they could eat.

Later on I became intrigued by a traffic cop standing on his box, waving his white-gloved hand frantically yet rhythmically in his tireless effort to keep some semblance of order at his assigned intersection where the streets came at him from all directions. I thought of "Candid Camera," when they showed a cop with his highly stylized approach to this same situation and set music to it.

Other than the heavy helicopter activity overhead and the high profile of the military, this could be any city in the world in the daylight. Huff and I never did find the hotel we were looking for, so a lot of our time was spent in areas geared strictly to the serviceman masses, with bars, girls, and loud rock 'n roll. Somebody must sell the plans for these areas all over the world — they're the same from San Diego to Hong Kong.

Saigon
Bicycle Cab

Austin DEUEL

Word came down to Dick and me of more trouble in the north, so we headed off to Dong Ha in a C-130. We knew it had something to do with the DMZ (Demilitarized Zone, which is a neutral fire zone). After checking in at the CIB tent in Dong Ha, we were told it was the first sweep of the war into the DMZ for the purpose of clearing out the North Vietnamese Army buildup in that supposedly neutral area. This action was named "Operation Hickory." Shaad and I went out to the helicopter pad to hitch a ride into the field. All departures were high priority so we waited for more than two hours. Cathy Leroy, who had a good nose for trouble, was there and also having no success in obtaining transportation. Shaad finally got tired of waiting and went back to the CIB tent. I decided to wait awhile longer and eventually caught the last chopper out. The door gunner advised me it was going to be a hot landing and emphasized the haste with which we must get off the chopper.

As we drew closer to the battle area and started to lose altitude, the door gunner braced himself, staring down the barrel of his machine gun. This was my first announced hot landing and I was nervous because I sat next to the door and was to be the first out. I'd had a lot of proof in the past that I was a clumsy oaf, and this was not an ideal position for one with my attributes. I only hoped I could move fast enough and not get hung up in the doorway, blocking the necessary rapid departure of the others. As we dropped out of the sky, the door gunner stiffened even more in anticipation of fire and my heart sank — the moment had come. I don't even remember going through the door. I do remember the fast approaching tree line. Pure instinct had my legs headed for it.

As I drew closer, someone in a foxhole looked up at me and said, "Oh, great. Just what we need."

He was reading the patch on my utility shirt that said "Combat Artist." With my pistol slapping my side, urging me on like a jockey's quirt, I was definitely no help in their situation which, I found out later, was not good.

I borrowed an entrenching tool and hastily dug a foxhole. When I had finished, I looked around me as night closed in and watched some young Marines trying to fix a tank that had lost its track to a mine twenty-five yards away. There were several other tanks parked along the tree line, their guns pointing out. It was like the Old West, with the wagons all drawn up in a circle for the night. As the last light hung on the horizon, a

81

sergeant ordered some Marines to take an axe to about twenty or thirty 50-gallon gasoline drums, letting their contents pour out on the ground in what seemed like a great waste to me. I was to understand the action later.

As darkness gained control, the outposts were set out and their reliefs assigned. There were no continuous night flares here as on Hill 881 South and my eyes strained to get used to the total blackness. There was a drum roll sound far off; this time Dong Ha and Con Thien were the origin. The snoring of exhausted men started to override the sound of the distant fire. I never thought of snoring as a giveaway noise for a position. Our artillery kept their harassing fire on the perimeter, constantly changing the pattern of fire so the enemy couldn't second-guess its impact.

In a foxhole next to me were a captain and two young Marines. They were on a first name basis and, from the tone of their conversation, had obviously been together for a long time. They passed the early part of the night in the sort of gentle, nervous conversation men exchange in a tight situation, talking of everything except where they were. Sleep finally overtook the young Marines, but the captain stayed up, sitting on the edge of the foxhole alone with his burden of command.

I was too scared to sleep so I figured for my own protection I'd better keep an eye on the captain. I didn't know his orders or plans of the operation. They could get up in the middle of the night and just leave. Nobody knew me, no one was aware of my presence or would miss me if they moved out in the dark.

Suddenly, there was a kettledrum roll off in the night that was different. Somebody shouted, "Incoming!", and the whole night erupted in explosions; falling pieces of dirt hit my helmet. It stopped as suddenly as it had begun and the quiet hung as heavily on the air as the smell of burnt gunpowder. Then the kettledrum rolled and it started all over again. Now I knew why they had destroyed the gasoline drums. It was to avoid adding destructive power to the enemy shells in case of a direct hit on them. After the third salvo, that haunting cry, "Corpsman!" shattered the brief silence.

Every incoming mortar sounded as if it was going to hit me on top of my head. I had squeezed the borrowed entrenching tool so hard that I bent the good-luck Marine Corps ring Larry had given to me before I left the States; it would eventually have to be cut off my finger. The mortars continued for about

an hour, then all went to black silence. I regained my position to observe the captain and watched him move from side to side in his foxhole, constantly changing the direction of his gaze. He definitely knew more than I did about what was going on so I matched his movements. Sometime during the night he got out of his foxhole and headed for the nearby tree line with me right on his heels, but he had just gone to take a leak. I felt stupid and embarrassed but I was not going to let him out of my sight!

Waiting for dawn under uncomfortable conditions is probably the hardest waiting men ever do. It's truly serving "dark time" when you're wet, cold and fearful, and the night is an eternity long. But morning finally did arrive and the men began forming up for the continuing push toward the DMZ. There was some incoming harassing fire, one or two mortar rounds every fifteen minutes or so.

As the battle heated up, I saw Cathy Leroy again, talking to a lieutenant colonel in her usual brash way. He was trying to maintain some manners in this insane place as she demanded a few Marines to escort her from our position to Con Thien which was in sight across the valley. He told her firmly that it was solid NVA in between and he would never see her or his Marines again if they attempted it. She was very upset and disrespectful of his situation, implying that the Marine Corps had nothing but a pair of soggy teabags for balls. But there was some justice: about an hour later, she was wounded by a mortar round and evacuated out of the area.

I looked at the men in the trees around me, the air overhead filled with the flight of small arms projectiles which left their sound behind as they passed overhead, punctuated by large explosions which could not be identified as incoming or outgoing due to the thick cover of the jungle. It seemed like a bad dream. Casualties were starting to mount, probably on both sides although I was only seeing the one side of it. My camera became inoperable due to the mud and dirt so I began helping with the wounded. I worked my way back to the Landing Zone and the captain I had been next to the night before passed by, slightly wounded, being fussed over by the young Marines who'd been at his side. Some of the wounded were now being brought in on ontosses and tanks. Due to the heavy mortar mixed with the small arms fire, we had a lot of amputees among the wounded.

I was helping a corpsman by giving him an extra pair of hands to hold plasma bags or whatever needed. At one point, he and I were loosening a tourniquet on a young Marine who'd had his leg blown off below the knee and as I stared into his face, I realized he didn't know yet that his leg was gone. I thought of what he would have to face the next day, being told his perfect nineteen-year-old body had been assaulted beyond repair, and what his family was going to have to go through: the telegram announcing that he'd been wounded but not that he'd lost a leg; that shock would come later.

He kept moaning over and over, "Get me out of here, get me out of here."

We heard the "whoop, whoop" of the approaching Medivac chopper heading for the LZ which was marked by the drifting smoke of a red smoke grenade indicating the pickup area for wounded.

The medic and I simultaneously grabbed the young Marine and headed for the chopper's anticipated landing spot. Just as it was about to settle down the last twenty feet, automatic weapon fire burst from the tree line behind us, aimed at the giant green bug of mercy. The pilot hit his collectors to change the pitch of the rotor blades and claw back to the safety of the sky. But there was still some loss of altitude before this maneuver became effective, giving us one shot at tossing the wounded Marine through the open door now ten feet or so above us. The door gunner stepped back, anticipating our effort. As the helicopter leaned away from us to gather speed for its climb, we let fly. The door gunner leaned down and grabbed the top of the wounded man's shirt so he wouldn't fall back out, then pulled him the rest of the way in. As they lifted off, I could see the good leg hanging down and the bloody shinbone of the other pointing helplessly off into space.

Dazed by this sight, I momentarily forgot my exposed position. The corpsman had already made it back to the tree line for cover when I started one of those runs where your whole life's ambition is two hundred feet.

The day continued along the same line. The resistance was very heavy and I overheard one Marine telling another why. It seems it was Ho Chi Minh's birthday and the enemy was "celebrating." Marine reinforcements were moving in, the wounded had all been evacuated, and when things started to settle down for awhile the Medivacs started taking out our dead. I caught

87

a chopper out on one of these missions. I no longer got sick at the sight of death — the mind seems to erect a barrier and the situation becomes dreamlike rather than real.

As I stepped down from the chopper at Dong Ha, I saw a 2½ ton truck with its tailgate down, waiting to top off its grisly load of freshly killed Marines. I silently helped the lone Marine complete his load of death with the three bodies from our chopper. A reporter rushed forward to take a picture but the driver chased him off. I stared at the truck. God! This looked like one of the photographs of a liberated concentration camp in Germany at the end of World War II, only they were in black and white and this was in vivid color. The driver and I lifted the gate of the truck and latched it shut and I stared after the cargo as he drove off across the runway; arms and legs were jiggling, blood was draining from the corners of the closed tailgate. What man does to man!

As I walked off to CIB, more sensitive in one way and hardened in another, I saw Shaad limping from a barefoot run to a bunker the night before during a rocket attack that had left dead and wounded here also.

My finger was hurting from the ring I had bent the night before, so I had the ring cut off. I reflected that it had been lucky for Larry in World War II. Now it was working on its second war!

I watched a sergeant going through the personal effects of a private who had been killed during his first twenty-four hours in this country. The sergeant was reading the mail the dead man had never received. He was from La Puente, California, where I had once lived myself before moving to the San Diego area. He was also married. I asked the sergeant why he was reading the mail and he told me they did it in the case of married men so the family back home wouldn't have the added pain of possibly learning through a forwarded letter that the dead man was having an extramarital affair. Reading a dead man's mail is a spooky job and I was surprised someone thought of that possible problem in the midst of all this insanity.

CHAPTER TWELVE

Operation Hickory was my last operation before going home, and I returned to CIB Da Nang and my painting routine, taking short trips around the countryside to observe the local people in their everyday struggles under the added burden of war. Those Vietnamese who survived to an old age showed such dignity and character. I was driving down a dirt road on the edge of Da Nang one day when a 2½ ton truck loaded in the back with Marines came toward me, its speed accentuated by a rooster tail of high rolling dust. There was the usual stream of Vietnamese walking along the side of the road, various loads balanced on their shoulders or heads. An older gentleman, bent by age, with a little wisp of a gray beard, dressed all in white and wearing the standard cone-shaped hat, was picking his way along with the help of a cane. The giant dust cloud rolled over him and as it settled down around his feet he turned slowly, lifting his head and pointing his arm at the rapidly disappearing chariot of war. Extending his middle finger, he waved after them disapprovingly for their rude violation of his world.

The technological spread between their way of doing things and ours was evident everywhere. True, some grease-covered kids were carrying batteries, generators and other motor parts here and there, trying to keep what few motors they had running. In contrast, I watched a man squatted on a thick plank, using a crosscut handsaw to cut it lengthwise. It was going to take quite awhile to complete this task that in one of our lumber yards would have taken only a few minutes. It was an antlike society — there was much activity everywhere you looked, but this effort produced little growth or progress. It just barely maintained a standard of living I'm sure hadn't changed much in a hundred years.

The prevalent religion was Buddhism and there were many little temples alongside the roads with incense burning, reminding me of the roadside chapels in Mexico with their lighted candles. They buried their dead above ground in an upright, fetal position, covering them with a mound of dirt. The first time I saw a concentration of these graves from the air, I asked the door gunner if there had been a B-52 raid in the area. He got a laugh out of that. The more affluent Vietnamese used concrete instead of dirt to cover their dead.

Even though this was a lush, green, water-filled country, the cattle and horses looked thin and bony; only the water buffaloes looked truly healthy, although pigs, ducks, and chickens did

91

well enough. But the horses and cows, in addition to being infested with internal parasites, were forced to graze on grass so tall it didn't have the nourishment that short, new grass does. I don't know what the Vietnamese would have thought if I'd told them we have doctors who work only on animals!

In the evenings I enjoyed watching the sunsets over the Da Nang River. Sampans would glide by with their human motors standing in the stern, rhythmically moving a single oar back and forth. A lone fisherman squatted on a barely exposed rock just offshore, patiently waiting for the last catch of the day. These scenes should have been on postcards in the lobby of the Da Nang Hilton Hotel for people to buy between their golf games and evening dining instead of in the middle of all the sounds of war. I did some fishing myself. I took a tablespoon from the club, cut off the handle and put a triple hook on it. When I did catch something, I never knew what it was going to look like until I landed it. To add to a fisherman's delight, I'm sure the fish had never seen a spoon in these parts either. There sure were a lot of beautiful fish in those waters.

They also had a lizard over there I would have given anything to bring home — the only talking lizard in the world, at least in English. It was definitely influenced by our arrival in its country. This lizard was about a foot and a half long and liked to lie on a tree limb at night, letting fly with its terrific command of the English language: "Fuck you, fuck you!"

During my Da Nang wanderings, I was invited to a celebration dinner with the Montagnard tribesmen working for the Green Berets stationed there. They were from the mountains of Vietnam and not liked by either the North or South Vietnamese. Every country seems to have a race of people who are the victims of prejudice, and usually they were there before those who hate them.

They were a warrior society and worked for the Green Berets as a mercenary army. They were trained, armed and paid by the Green Berets. The Montagnards started training their boys at the age of eight; they went on operations at twelve with a weapon for battle. To keep them in Da Nang, the Green Berets had to bring their families with them and provide for them also.

When I arrived at their camp, it was bustling with the activity of preparation for the celebration. They had two cows, one tied or, in cowboy terms, "sidelined" to one of our water buffaloes, which is military terminology for a metal tank on wheels to

Looking Across The River From CIB

93

hold drinking water. Standing before this pitiful creature, dressed in a wrap-around orange robe, was a Buddhist priest, both hands on the grip of a Samurai sword, chanting and making intermittent slashes and stabs at the bellowing cow. He avoided a death stroke to keep the heart pumping as long as possible to aid those collecting blood from the wounds. They finally cut the cow's head off and finished butchering it for supper. They prepared the meat by boiling it in giant vats, with millions of flies doing touch-and-go on any parts floating on top.

Everyone was very excited about the feast that lay before them. Two long tables faced each other along opposite sides of an open-sided building which had a corrugated tin roof to protect it from the sun. In the center of each table was the severed head of a cow surrounded by pans of the animal's blood. This put forth a very distinctive smell that delighted the swarming flies. I sat down with the sergeant who had brought me to this fine event. The temperature was over 100 degrees, and before me there was hot beer and this plate supporting a hunk of meat that was white from the boiling process of its preparation. I then looked at our centerpiece looking back at me, fly-decorated tongue hanging out, its vacant eyes seeming to dare me to go ahead and take a bite.

I turned to the sergeant and said, "Boy, I can't wait to get home and open up a chain of this kind of restaurant!"

After the meal they formed up in ranks. The leaders made speeches and gave out awards to those who had done well in the operation they were celebrating; those that received the awards were very proud. Their Green Beret counterparts were sporting their Montagnard bracelets. These were made of a circle of thick brass and had to be squeezed on by another person; they were given as a mark of bravery to those who did well in battle.

My afternoon and evening with the Montagnards gave me another glimpse of a seldom seen culture. I returned to CIB thinking of the extremes of Vietnamese culture: from Ky with his starched black uniform, white scarf, and pearl-handled pistols to a barefooted farmer standing in muddy water with no modern machinery to help in his struggle to eke a living from his land.

CHAPTER THIRTEEN

It finally came time to go home. Though my tour in Vietnam had been short compared to most, my emotions were similar to those of anyone going home. You want to go so bad, but are saddened to leave the military friendships you have made, especially those made under combat conditions. You are even saddened to see those friends go home before you. It's a bond built under a tremendous need to survive and to break it makes you feel you are deserting those you leave behind under fire.

I turned in what I had to turn in and went to the Da Nang Airport at 0700 to catch the C-130 for Okinawa. As it turned out, the plane had engine trouble and we had to wait until one engine was taken off and replaced with another. We finally left at dark, my feet resting on the sick engine that sat in the middle of the plane for us to stare at all the way to Okinawa. We landed at Henderson Field on the Marine base on Okinawa at three o'clock in the morning.

As always, I was trying to get the jump on the military system, and thought that since I had different orders I could just go over to Kadena Airport on the other side of the island and catch the next flight to the United States. I grabbed a cab and made a run for it — to no avail and some laughter. I had to return to Henderson and go through their program. By the time I returned, the guys I'd come with were already processed. I stepped into the quonset hut where two Marines in white T-shirts were leaning on a counter. They told me to strip and dump my seabags on the floor, then giggled as they took away all the war souvenirs I wasn't supposed to have.

I finally gathered myself up and repacked. It was now four-thirty in the morning and still dark. I asked the two corporals where to go to catch up with my group. Everything in the military is abbreviated and I was never up on all their meanings, plus I had never been to Henderson before, so I had no idea where they tried to send me. I walked awhile, then just took a guess, entered a barracks and lay down on a bunk in the dark to get some sleep. I no sooner lay down than the lights came on and a sergeant started screaming at me to get up! From my prone position I looked up at shiny faces, crisp haircuts, and brilliant white T-shirts. I told myself they had sure cleaned up in a hurry as I lay there in jungle utilities, boots and a wrinkled green T-shirt, a day's growth of beard on my face. The sergeant paused in front of my rack to give me his personal attention since I hadn't moved yet. I got up grudgingly, to say the least,

GOING HOME ?

97

stumbled out into the darkness again and joined the formation that was brought to attention with a snap. The sergeant started to walk down the ranks, sending those he pointed to off to get brooms and other cleaning materials.

He got to me and I raised my hand in resistance and said, "Just a minute, is this the way you treat guys just coming out of Vietnam? This is terrible!"

After my speech, the sergeant looked at me and replied, "You idiot, these are the guys who are going."

After I arrived where I was supposed to be, my living conditions vastly improved. I spent a little over a week there before my flight to the States. We were inspected in our summer dress uniform for the last time and they checked our seabags and put customs seals on them. During the inspection, the gunny sergeant was trying to assure everyone that the welcome at home wasn't as bad as some of the rumors, although he did admit it wasn't all flowers. One of the rumors was that a couple of Marines in uniform had been beaten up at the Los Angeles airport, and there were demonstrations everywhere. The rumors flying around added to our anxiety about going home. Everyone was nervous about their reception by the American public, not knowing what was true and what was not. Some paired up as far as they could on their journey home and discussed the soonest they thought they could get rid of their uniforms. What a way to have to think coming home from a war your country sent you to fight!

The flight home was long and silent, with most of us lost in deep thought. The stewardesses were not as harassed by the prodding of young men as had happened on the flight over. This was a time for reflecting on experiences — probably the first time they had really thought about them.

We landed at Travis Air Force Base near San Francisco for another interminable military procedure. Air Force medics boarded the plane and checked our shot cards for the thousandth time. We finally took off for the last part of our flight to El Toro Marine Corps Air Base in southern California, beginning our descent over the Laguna hills with their big houses and backyard pools — they hadn't changed since I last saw them but I sure had! As the Continental 707 drew closer to the runway it suddenly jerked and swayed and everyone stiffened in silence. There was a thrust of the engines as they were given full power and we lifted back up into the sky and came around

for another try.

The look on everyone's face said, "Not now — don't mess up now!"

The second attempt was successful and we deplaned onto American soil. For most, it was the first time in over a year. We passed through Customs fast and quickly began to disperse in our many directions. My wife and children were supposed to be waiting there, especially since they lived just a little more than an hour away and the plane had a scheduled landing every day at this time. I passed the group readying to board for the return flight to Vietnam and went to the parking lot. There was no one there so I found a small patch of grass and lay down to wait.

My wife drove up more than an hour later — I can't remember the reason she was late although I'm sure it wasn't deliberate. But it pointed out to me the fact that even close relatives preferred to treat the homecoming from this war as just another routine arrival. I hugged her and the kids and we proceeded to drive home, she talking nervously and I distant and numb. Later, in my first contact with my mother, father, and sister, after all the "Hello's" and "How are you's," the real questions went unasked. They didn't know what to say to me or I to them. It was like trying to talk to a woman who has had a mastectomy. Everyone knew about it but you only wanted her to know you realized she was sick, not where or show any knowledge of what disfigurement she had incurred.

I was still on active duty for a time after I got home but I only went out to Camp Pendleton once in awhile to check in. They let me work in my studio at home. The physical war was over for me now but the internal sifting of my experiences continued like a coffeemaker dripping away. The process was going to take many painful and confusing years.

WELCOME HOME ?

I had had major shows at my gallery the last couple of years that included hundreds of different artists along with those I showed regularly. This was going to be my third year of this and I had always had a special kind of art show using the showroom for which I had designed unique lighting. This year I decided to bring the Marine Combat Art Show, with my work included, from Washington, D.C. I had some of Colonel Stiff's and Lieutenant Dermontt's work, along with some of the other artists in the program and I added some paintings I had done after I got home. This was probably the first public showing of art from Vietnam. It was August, 1967, and we had the Marine Corps Band from Pendleton as well as some fine young Marines in their dress blues to act as ushers for this event.

We had more than 25,000 people come to the art show. When they went through the military part, there was not much verbal reaction, just curiosity. This was quite a contrast to the high emotions I was to witness with the same subject fourteen years later in New York City.

When I first got home I did a lot of TV show interviews and many newspaper articles appeared based on my unusual job as a Marine Combat Artist in Vietnam. Some of my comments in the shows and articles were upsetting the applecart as far as some of the higher-ups in the military were concerned. My remarks were in no way negative about the performance of the Marine Corps. I had nothing but high praise for their efforts as a fighting unit, saying they were the finest young men our country had ever sent off to war. But the war sucked, with its political rope tying the hands of a military effort which was in itself political. I felt the purpose of our presence there was not clear. The Marine Corps became upset with some of my comments and tried to influence me to temper my remarks on the war and my exposure of the problems with the M-16.

On one occasion, I was about to go to Los Angeles and do the Joe Pine show. During the sixties, Pine was a headhunter for all the wrongs, especially those of the system. Just before leaving, I received a telephone call from Marine Corps Headquarters in Washington from a colonel I didn't know and whose name eludes me now. He advised me that I had to watch what I was saying to the news media, that my comments would hurt the Marine Corps. His voice was calm and he was calling me by my first name — that's when you know you are really in trouble with a superior ranking officer. They were trying to get

a handle on me, knowing a short-time PFC doesn't live in fear of his career being damaged or all the other military style control. He was trying kindness as a last resort. He kept saying that my statements could hurt the Marine Corps' ability to get the needed appropriation for their war effort.

I replied, "It's not when there's a war, it's when we're at peace that you're fighting to get your slice of a limited defense budget for your peacetime training maneuvers or keep the landing beaches at Pendleton from going public in their use. Besides that, I'm not a general so I doubt if my opinion has much weight."

Then he tried another attack plan and said I was just being emotional about my experiences.

I said, "You're darn right. People are dying and somebody's got to say something."

Then came a new tack which was the military one: "Well, that just wasn't what you saw!"

I snapped back, "When I first joined the Marine Corps in boot camp I listened to all the tales of Okinawa, Tarawa, Guadalcanal, Pork Chop Hill, and Chosan Reservoir in Korea where the Marines walked a hundred miles to the sea under the guns of the enemy every step and didn't leave one dead or wounded man behind in snow and ice. I believed them. I was at Hill 881, not you, and I expect you to believe me."

The conversation ended and I went off to do the Joe Pine show feeling torn because I love the Marine Corps and the history its many brave men have built. I didn't want to damage that in any way. I did the show and, fortunately, Pine was on my side. This was the most intense man I have ever met in my life; if he was out to get you, he could make verbal dogmeat out of you. I had seen him do it before to men who were smarter and better informed than I.

After the show I was in the restroom relieving my nervousness when he stomped in and went up to a urinal near me. He gave me a quick look and said, "I was a Marine," then made a fist with his left hand and thumped his wooden leg, pulled up his zipper and left without another word, as abruptly as he had come in.

I had one more encounter with the powers-that-be and it was over one of my paintings. The painting was "Even God Is Against Us." All the work I had done in Vietnam had been sent directly to Colonel Henri in Washington but this one I had done after I came home, so I sent him a photograph of it. He advised

SENT THIS CARTOON
TO THE WASHINGTON POST
WHEN THEY PUT CALLEY
ON TRIAL FOR HIS ACTIONS
IN VIETNAM

me that the painting could not be exhibited to the public yet; he felt they were not ready for such explicit combat art. It was one of my favorite paintings of my Vietnam effort and I felt saddened that it would be buried. I held it back even though technically it belonged to the Marine Corps since I had painted it while still on active duty. I eventually sold it to Eric Harvey who donated it to a museum in Calgary, Canada. Maybe the United States Government will give it amnesty some day. The Marine Corps did give me a little flak over it, but they didn't want to make a big media deal out of it so they dropped the subject but barred me as a listed combat artist for them which was too bad. I always wanted to go back to Parris Island and add a mural in the movie theater there about Vietnam since they had murals depicting major Marine Corps battles in all the other wars.

After being home awhile, sitting out the war with the rest of stateside America, I became silent and expressed little opinion on the war unless directly questioned. I had been home about five months when I attended a special high school reunion for George School. It was set up on the west coast for ex-students living in the area to meet the new dean since the school was located in the east. This event took place in Hollywood, which was easy for me to reach. Since it was a private Quaker boarding school, I was going to avoid acknowledging my recent experiences in southeast Asia. I knew their reactions would definitely be very negative and shocked. All of the men and women, except a very few like myself, were graduates of the east's finest Ivy League schools. The professions represented were mainly three: lawyers, doctors, and teachers, and all of the teachers seemed to be on sabbatical or just finishing one somewhere in the world to add to their doctorates.

When they had their formal meeting to discuss problems of the day and what to do about them, the first big question was what was George School doing to maintain the government-required racial equality, and did the number of minority groups attending George School come up to the regulated percentage. With the school's academic requirements, this was difficult — and, of course, every poor family has $12,000 extra to send a child to school! My class graduated in 1957 and Julian Bond was in it, but he was the only black in it and he met all the academic requirements.

The other serious discussion was on the public display of an

Army helicopter in a shopping mall where kids were allowed to climb on it and sit behind the guns, and how shocking that was and the damage it was doing by popularizing violence.

Visions of Vietnam went through my head. I pictured the room filled with the men and women of a Vietnamese village saying, "What's a shopping mall?" I thought of their very real problems and shook my head. This was insane. Some of these people were classmates of mine. I remembered when they tied on black armbands in 1956 and marched on the United Nations to ban the bomb. Now in their late twenties and early thirties, with all their education, their interest in earth-shaking problems had certainly narrowed.

I think one of the greatest comments on the war, all those years to its end, that didn't hurt your brain or call for a comment of "Bullshit!", was made on TV during a news program. I sat one night watching the latest pictures and the news from Vietnam, as usual filled with how bad and brutal the American soldier was in his acts of barbarism on the battlefield, perpetuating the Ugly American image. A cameraman and a reporter were following an operation in the Delta, obviously a search and destroy mission. A young private was standing at the edge of a rice paddy. An armored personnel carrier had just sped past him, its tracks tearing at the mud beneath the surface. It was making its journey to the other side and through the dike to the next paddy, totally destroying the ability of the dike to contain the water so necessary to grow the rice. The reporter shoved his microphone in the private's very young face and asked, "What do you think of all this?"

The soldier started desperately looking around for someone of higher authority nearby to talk for him. I'm sure he'd been told he'd be in big trouble if he talked to the press.

The reporter persisted. "You can talk. What do you really think of all this?"

The private took one last frantic look for help, but none was in sight. Then, with his slight body holding up more equipment that it should have had to, his pencil-thin neck making his helmet look oversized for his proportions and needs, his eyes darting quickly from side to side, he said in a slow, soft voice, "Oh, man! I just don't like driving through these people's gardens!"

Out of the mouths of babes!

CHAPTER FIFTEEN

The years went by and I picked up my life and buried the memories but the Vietnam conflict refused to die for me as it refused to die for all. The emotional changes came gradually as I closed in on the collision course between what I had seen in southeast Asia and the reception at home. Such personal conflicts were happening all around us, some on the front pages of newspapers, but most private and known only to the immediate family of the veteran involved. When a conflict came to its conclusion on the TV evening news, it was explained that the Vietnam experience had nothing to do with this individual's problem of adjusting to society and its rules. I'm sure it wasn't the only reason for most of the incidents where a veteran came to a tragic end but it certainly was a big contributor to the straw that broke his back.

The returning veteran had to find within himself the worth and merit so widely denied by his fellow citizens. He had to overcome the internal cold and numbness in order to regain his confidence and reinstate his emotional life. And he had to do this while all around him the rhetoric and national events continued to make his personal effort in Vietnam seem of less and less value as time went on.

This climate of opinion set him apart from the veterans of all other wars this country had fought. Members of the VFW, confused and frustrated by the Vietnam war, felt he was not the fighting man they had been — he had "lost the war." During this period of isolation, the term "Brother" was used among the returning Vietnam veterans as a greeting of understanding and a bond in their loneliness. This led to the creation of their own VFW to provide some peace and a less judgmental atmosphere than they found in the other VFW.

Those professional soldiers who played the game of politics instead of war stayed on in the service and raised their ranks; other officers and high-ranking NCO's quit in disgust and confusion. Politics caused the Vietnam warriors to further question their purpose when amnesty was given to those who had fled to Canada to avoid their country's call. The men who went to Vietnam were unaware they had a choice when their country demanded they expose themselves to hostile fire with the chance of death or loss of limb. Who gives amnesty to those who have lost an arm or leg, or who will spend the rest of their lives in a VA hospital with death their only means of checking out? It makes suckers out of those who sacrificed so much.

There should have been some requirement for those who sat out the war in Canada to spend time in the Peace Corps or some other government service.

Even the memorial in Washington, D.C. turned into a political battle, disregarding the wishes of the veterans themselves. The artist's wishes became more important than those of the men for whom it was intended. The young girl's design that was chosen and paid for — the black "V" in the ground with the names of all the dead on it — was okay, but the Vietnam veterans unanimously wanted to add a three-dimensional sculpture in the center of the "V" to give it more visual relation to the war. The artist screamed foul. Her artistic concept was not to be changed — it would damage the integrity of her design. This was not an art show! It was to honor millions of those who served and paid the price, and their wishes should have come before those of the artist. The Memorial Commission did commission Hart to do three figures, a very nice piece, but it was placed off to the side — cut off again. The Vietnam veterans can't even have their own memorial the way they want it.

The politicians even allowed a movie star to go to the enemy's camp, creating stress and pain for those who had no control over their situation, and causing those who refused to be exhibited to suffer torture, solitary confinement, and humiliation. These men were in an enemy prison as the result of defending her right of free speech, her right to speak out against the war — but at home, not in the enemy's camp. She should at least not have been allowed back into the United States until the war was over and the prisoners, too, could go home — if they lived. I don't think that during World War II the government would have allowed Bob Hope to visit a German or Japanese prisoner-of-war camp and expound on the unjustness of his country's war effort, then return to the United States!

By the early 1980's, the quality of the Vietnam veterans' efforts was becoming more widely acknowledged, as was the injustice of their homecoming mistreatment. And the veteran himself was coming to grips with his experience and placing it in the right emotional file cabinet. Many of us were passing through our final negative approach to a productive life: heavy drinking and other self-destructive habits and courses we'd been following for years.

I was still heading down this road when I was called by a fellow veteran I didn't know, Dick Stranberg, who had com-

manded a river boat on the Delta for the Navy. He was looking for professional artists who were also Vietnam veterans to put a show together for Veterans Day in November, 1981, in St. Paul and Minneapolis. I don't know how he found me but he asked if I would be interested in the event and I said yes.

My first piece was a small sculpture titled, "For What? Hill 881 South." In the process of doing it, I called Dick and said I was having great emotional difficulty over the project; in fact, it was the first time I'd cried about the war and I can't sculpt very well through tears. I also went through photos I had taken in Vietnam and hadn't looked at in years. I did finally finish the sculpture as well as some paintings. One of these was another "Even God Is Against Us" which was used to open the Walter Cronkite news show's acknowledgement of our art show, "The Vietnam Experience," followed by other fine works of art. The response in Minneapolis-St. Paul was nice, but quiet.

Months later we took the show to the Big Apple — New York City. A fellow veteran by the name of Bernie Elderman, a writer, organized a drive to raise much-needed funds for shipping works in from all over the country and revamping the aviary at the Central Park Zoo into an art gallery for our show. With much effort and Dick Stranberg's expertise gained from putting on the show in Minneapolis, we made ready for opening night. There was art of all types and styles, and of as high a caliber as I had ever shown with. We had tapes of poetry and music of the sixties and early seventies playing, and there were photographs and a continuous slide show. As the hour of our opening approached, Dick, Bernie and I, along with some of the other artists, stood staring at the crowd that was waiting for the doors to open. Bernie looked at me and said, "This is New York so I don't know if we're going to get a hundred leftover hippies attacking with spray cans or a Vietnam veteran freaking out with an M-16."

We opened the doors and the crowd spilled in. The reaction was unbelievably warm and emotional. We heard comments such as, "It's about time. Now I know what my brother went through." And those who had been there themselves renewed acquaintance with places they recognized. There was the well-dressed veteran with his family, showing familiar sights to his kids who hadn't yet been born when he first had seen them. Veterans were hugging other veterans they'd brought in wheelchairs. It was the first large-scale, positive reaction I'd seen in

the fourteen years since I'd been home from Vietnam. The wounds were beginning to heal.

The show was seen by well over twenty thousand people, surpassing any of our expectations, and the positive reactions were also totally unexpected.

CHAPTER SIXTEEN

The Vietnam veteran on the whole is not seeking pity but only understanding and respect given to veterans of past wars our country has fought in the defense of freedom and human rights regardless of the status of those defended. There are those still living a troubled existence and using the Vietnam experience as the total reason for their problems. All veterans have had some sorts of problems as a result of their individual experiences in Vietnam; they are as different as the number of men and women who went to southeast Asia. Most of them have worked those problems out, with damage done only to themselves and their loved ones. They have learned to place the painful experience into the right psychological category in their minds to free themselves of the destructive emotions that had hold on them at one time or another.

There was self-pity but also another emotion that usually first hit you in Vietnam. By the time you arrived home, you were pissed off and frustrated by the magnitude of all the wrongs of the war and the range of its victims. The little things added up to big things which started with the actual war itself, and those feelings continued when you got home.

A friend of mine, Bill Stensland, a Marine Corps captain at the time, had a command on top of a hill called Con Thien until he was wounded and removed for repairs. This bleak pile of red, usually muddy earth was located just below the DMZ and it was an outpost of hell, a continual impact area for the North Vietnamese artillery. The men were up to their necks in thick, red mud, bailing out their holes between the incoming artillery rounds that continued until dark, then passed into a cold silence only to resume by dawn's early light.

A small thing like a candle became a big deal in the midst of this daily misery, but their repeated requests for a fresh supply of candles went unfilled; all they received was a communique that no candles were available. Yet the new replacements for the dead and wounded always had brand-new candles, thoughtfully given to them by the supply sergeant from his personal inventory — for just one dollar, of course. So here was a captain, up to his ass in mud and casualties, trying to keep himself and his men alive and do his military duty in the war, having to sit down in the middle of all this shit and write Command that somebody was stealing his candles. Where he and his men were, they didn't have old Batman movies or clubs for nighttime entertainment. A candle was the only light they had to write

letters home or read paperback books to help pass the dark hours of their time in hell.

This sort of problem could happen in any war and probably did. Veterans of earlier wars could relate to a few problems of this nature. But there were many that could not. And because of this, the system had more trouble characterizing this war for the public than it did in the past. The many and varied attempts at capturing the Vietnam war in the movies have all failed in the eyes of most veterans. There were bits and pieces that came close, but it's a hard movie to make because this war's purpose was not as clear as it had been in other wars. John Wayne tried the old-fashioned "Sands of Iwo Jima" approach in "The Green Berets" and fell short to the point of being laughable in the eyes of most veterans, oversimplifying a war that was complex and full of extremes. "Apocalypse Now" tried a way-out approach and had its moments as did "The Deer Hunter." Most recently, "Platoon," which was created by a Vietnam veteran, still falls short by far. They all portray the untrue Vietnam stigma of pot-smoking, baby-killing infantrymen in the field, wearing bandannas and lots of jewelry around their necks (instead of dogtags wrapped in black tape for quiet and no reflection), of inept officers either poorly trained or crazy, and of the average soldier as a high school dropout and cannon fodder for the rich. In truth, the troops in Vietnam had the highest average education level of those in any previous war. The units were military in discipline and dress, and did not sit in bunkers openly smoking marijuana through water pipes. This sort of thing did go on, but the level was in proportion to the involvement of the men in the war: higher for those manning typewriters than those using machine guns.

The inferiority of character, the lack of morals, the poor level of intelligence, these were occurring at the top level of both the military and in Washington. That's why the war is so confusing. The quality was at the bottom and the everyday soldier's screams for common sense and obvious right were drowned in the pool of power at the top. The press, and now a fellow veteran in a movie, portray the Vietnam veteran with the taint of disgrace in his actions. It's as if he'd been left alone over there to make all those moral decisions himself about whom to kill, and if he ran out of the obvious, he grabbed the nearest kid or mama-san between killing the ducks and pigs.

All these events and actions of the Vietnam era and post-era

have diminished the pride of those who served our country when they were called upon. It created tension at that time which could be seen in this country's various uniformed military when they walked in small numbers in public.

I was reminded of this just recently when I walked into a very nice restaurant. As I passed through the dining room, I saw a young Marine corporal sitting in his dress blues, his chest covered with fresh rows of ribbons from the recent Lebanon campaign. His girlfriend was obviously very proud to be seen there with a man in uniform. Other people in the restaurant were looking at the handsome young couple with appreciation; respect and support were shown in their glances. My heart sank as I looked at him sitting there with the pride of a young warrior returned from the battlefield of a just cause. It saddened me to realize that the Vietnam soldier returning from his battlefield would have been at risk in the same situation. His presence would probably have divided the restaurant as discussions of America's Southeast Asia policy heated up at the individual tables, the remarks spilling over in his direction as to his personal responsibility for the death and destruction he must have dealt out over there. Those opposed to the policy would have said how sick he was for being a part of it and how ashamed he should be.

It made me feel good to see the pride in the uniform shown mutually and openly by the young man and the diners.

CHAPTER SEVENTEEN

The energy generated by the shows in New York and Minneapolis nurtured my little bronze into a twice-lifesize memorial destined for placement near one of the finest examples of the patriotism of "so few for so many" — The Alamo in San Antonio, Texas. This all came to pass because those involved in its concept and being were Vietnam veterans: John D. Baines (whose arrival in Vietnam is described in an earlier chapter), the driving force and the man who commissioned the piece, served two tours, one as a Navy Seal; Glen Kirkpatrick, who made the arrangements for the truck to haul the memorial and finished his truck driving career with this last load, served two tours in Force Recon USMC; and countless other veterans assisted.

My second personal battle for Hill 881 South started January 1, 1986, when I began working on the memorial sculpture. I was to weld over 5,000 feet of cold-rolled steel for its armature, and apply more than 20,000 pounds of plaster to be ground and filed to form 170 pieces of bronze that would be welded together. The finished sculpture weighed 10,670 pounds. Scheduled dedication date was November 9, 1986, and there were ten months of strain, both mental and physical, for myself and my fellow workers. All this work was done in Scottsdale, Arizona, and we did meet our deadline, loading the sculpture onto the back of a huge flatbed truck for its 975-mile journey down a twentieth century "Trail of Tears" for its dedication in San Antonio.

You are never aware of who has been touched by the Vietnam war until a project such as this is started. I've known John and Ann DiTommaso in the art business for years. They stumbled onto this project in its final days of completion, when Ann told me that her brother was a PFC in the Marine Corps and from Texas and was killed May 7, 1967, about the same time of the battles for Hills 881 South and North. After that, Ann came every day until the memorial's final loading on the truck to head for its permanent home in San Antonio. She gave me, Glen and Bobby (the other truck driver) each a small yellow rose, then tied a yellow ribbon to the memorial and gave me one large rose for her brother. I told her I would put it under the sculpture's final resting place for him. We had no idea this was just the beginning of our trail of tears.

The outpouring of emotion on this trip came as a great surprise to Glen and me. The memorial seemed to lance a nasty boil for its viewers, releasing the emotional pus of past years

for a final time and destroying the suppressive grip the Vietnam war had on our lives. We who were involved in the memorial's beginning hoped its importance would be seen and felt, but what was happening was beyond our wildest thoughts. After so many years of stifled emotions, the outpouring was spontaneous and heartfelt.

Glen said it best: "Its title should be 'Truth' which was so lacking in Vietnam!"

We stopped that first night at the Toltec 76 truck stop in Elroy, Arizona. "Eloy" in Spanish means land of the forsaken. The owner allowed us a prestigious spot for parking the truck for viewing and insisted on feeding us dinner and breakfast. Glen couldn't sleep; he kept an all-night vigil with the memorial. By morning, it was streaming with yellow ribbons that had been added during the night. One truck driver went into the gift shop during the night and, upon discovering they were out of yellow ribbons, bought three yellow T-shirts to tear into additional ribbons to tie on in the memory of a loved one or friend. Written messages and money were also left during the night, some with just a name or a few words such as "we miss you."

One remembering note found in the new day's light read:

> "We called you Little Feather,
> you were our friend.
> Your body is gone now,
> but your spirit lives on
> inside this statue.
> You live still,
> and in our hearts
> you always will.
> I miss you, Ben.
>> Sgt. Ben J. Hogan (Little Feather)
>> Missing in Action, August, 1970"

Glen and I cried along with so many others on this trip to San Antonio. As we drove further, more sorrows were tied to the monument, now streaming with yellow tears. Even at night its magic could not be hidden by darkness or our speed.

At one point, the CB screeched with a man's voice saying, "Where are you going, woman?"

A woman's voice replied, "Did you see that statue?"

He asked, "What statue?"

"The one on that red Peterbilt," she said. "I'm going to get a better look."

Her 18-wheeler pulled alongside and slowed, followed by her bewildered fellow trucker.

Glen, who was running the front door in my pickup, broke in with his deep, slow Texas drawl, "That's the Vietnam war memorial for Alamo City."

The woman truck driver said, "I was a medic for five years — 1967 to 1972."

Glen answered, "You might've taken care of me, darlin'!"

She said, "I only took care of Marines."

"I was a Marine," Glen announced.

She replied, with sadness in her voice, "There were so many, I wouldn't remember."

Then she added, "That statue has a lot of feeling. Whoever did it was there. Well, I'm going to Florida but when I get to Alamo City, I'll look it up."

Glen said, "You do that. We all love you, darlin'," as the tail lights of her truck disappeared into the darkness of the New Mexico night.

Glen, Bobby, and I still were not prepared for the events of the next day as we penetrated deep into Texas. I was riding beside Bobby in the truck with Glen running the front door position. The monument was behind us on the trailer, its patina of fresh morning dew drying by the winds of our journey. I looked out over the hood of our bright fire engine red Peterbilt, its twin stacks straining with the roar of the engine, their shiny chrome surfaces reflecting the soft colors of the Texas dawn breaking before us on the flat horizon. I thought of the events of the past eleven months of work to complete this memorial and the twenty years of pain for millions of other Vietnam veterans and their families which was the reason for its being.

As we approached the turnoff on I-10 to San Antonio, the most desolate part of the trip, other 18-wheelers requested we pull up at the rest stop just before the turnoff so they could have a better look. We pulled in with a dozen trucks peeling off behind us and parked at an angle across the truck area. The trucks lined up for a look, standing there like giant caterpillars, their headlights creating a haunting stare. A cool West Texas breeze blew briskly over the area and there was nothing as far as the eye could see. The quiet was disturbed by the easy idle of those giant diesels tapping out their patient wait as their drivers gathered around for a look-see. One driver was accompanied by his brother who was obviously his constant compan-

Vietnam War Memorial, San Antonio

129

ion. The brother was blind and the driver guided him over to the lowboy trailer that was the monument's temporary pedestal, helped him onto it and then to the bronze to allow him to "see" it with his hands. There wasn't a dry eye in the place. A woman truck driver walked up to me, grabbed my hand, and with a comforting squeeze said, "Thanks."

Glen, Bobby, and I gathered ourselves, as we had so many times, to head down the final stretch to Alamo City. We arrived the next morning in misty rain and by that afternoon the memorial was in its final resting place.

Sunday, November 9, was the date of the unveiling and I was surrounded by friends, family, and the great spirit of the Alamo. I met my foxhole buddy, now Sergeant Major Dick Shaad (until this event I hadn't known if he'd lived through his next tour), and Don Hossack (the radioman depicted on the memorial), who was wounded on the hill and the only radioman to survive, now a detective in Kalispell, Montana. There were the usual speeches by dignitaries and two jet fly-bys. Then, as a squad of Marines in full combat gear pulled the covering off the monument, came that familiar sound, the far-off "whoop-whoop-whoop" that pulses in your ears. Suddenly, a formation of Hueys appeared overhead, with the radioman on the monument looking up at them. I didn't think I had any more tears in me, but they came!

Then the crowd surged in for a closer look, veterans openly crying and hugging one another, placing their medals on the monument. The bouquet of flowers increased by the minute, along with American flags, notes, photographs. This continued for days. I tried to go back for a moment by myself later but even at 2:30 in the morning, small groups of people were still there.

I've been through some great highs in the art world and some special moving moments because of public reaction to my work, such as the 1982 opening of "The Vietnam Experience" in New York City. But to have something I had created turn from being a piece of art to being an altar, as happened in San Antonio, is moving beyond my powers of description.

Glen had made one last early morning visit to the memorial and I met him there to say goodbye.

"It just rained a little bit," he said. "Austin, you won't believe it. It cries!"

I had finally completed and laid to rest my assignment as a Marine Corps combat artist.

DEATH AT MY DOOR

DAY IS OVER AS DANGER HASTENS
YOUNG MARINES AT THEIR BATTLE STATIONS
INSTRUMENTS OF WAR OUTLINE THE SKY
MEANS OF DEATH ARE STANDING BY

CAN IT BE TRUE ON THIS HIGH HILL
FORCES WILL CLASH ONLY TO KILL?
SILENCE FILLS THE NEAR MOONLESS NIGHT
RESTLESS THOUGHTS OF A BLOODY FIGHT

SOMEWHERE THROUGH THE DARKNESS CREEPING
A DATE WITH DEATH IS IN THE KEEPING
ALONE I SIT AND QUESTION WHY
LIFE ITSELF TO BE BORN TO MERELY DIE?

DAVID G. ROGERS 1ST LT. USMC
APRIL 30, 1967
HILL 881 SOUTH, REPUBLIC OF VIETNAM

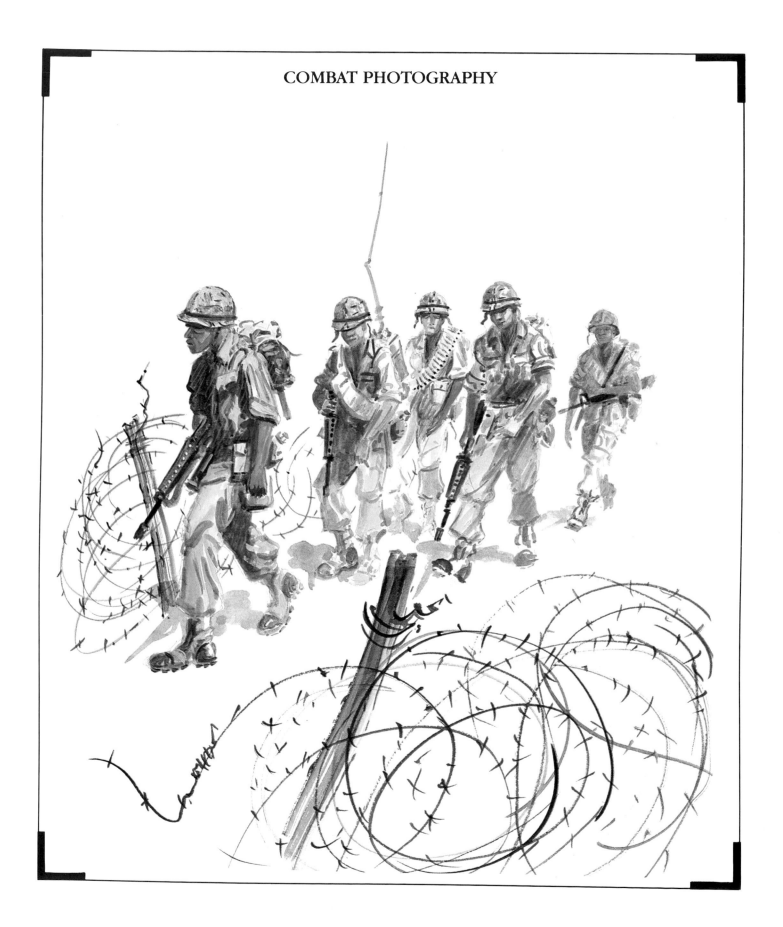

138

BIOGRAPHY

Austin Deuel has won innumerable awards for watercolor, oil and bronze sculpture in many major Southwestern art shows since 1966.

His work is in the permanent collection of museums from Canada to Washington, D.C. His work has also appeared on calendars, greeting cards, and magazine covers for years.

While serving in the USMC he served in Vietnam in 1967 as a combat artist. Some of these experiences have travelled with an art show in the past few years called "THE VIETNAM EXPERIENCE" which has been well received in New York City and many other large cities in the United States. He was commissioned to do a heroic size bronze sculpture representing his experiences in Vietnam which is placed in the city of San Antonio as the Vietnam War Memorial.

VIETNAM
EVEN GOD IS AGAINST US
EDITED AND DESIGNED BY GAIL CROSS

POEM: DEATH AT MY DOOR BY DAVID G. ROGERS, 1ST LT. USMC

PHOTOGRAPHIC CREDITS
COMBAT PHOTOGRAPHY BY AUSTIN DEUEL
VIETNAM WAR MEMORIAL BY BUD SHANNON
COURTESY OF JOHN D. BAINES
VIETNAM VETERANS MEMORIAL OF SAN ANTONIO INC.
ART PHOTOGRAPHY BY B. DICKERSON
PHOTOGRAPHY USED IN COLLAGE, SYMBOLS OF 1967
FROM LIFE MAGAZINE, OCTOBER 20, 1967